Savanting

Outperforming your Potential

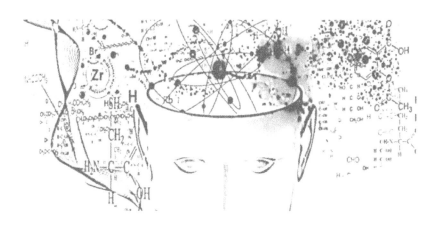

Lauren Holmes

    Published by Frontiering
    www.frontiering.com

Dedicated to those seeking self-actualization,
self-transcendence and beyond to leave
their most impactful footprint on our world

SAVANTING – Outperforming your Potential

CONTENTS

III SIGNS OF SAVANTING

V SAVANTING TO MAN'S HIGHEST GOALS

CONTENTS

PREFACE

*I don't believe that consciousness is generated by the
brain. I believe that the brain is more of a receiver of
consciousness.*   Graham Hancock

*S*avanting: Outperforming your Potential reveals an unprecedented protocol for creativity, ingenuity, self-actualization, self-transcendence, and even cosmic consciousness. It empowers noncreatives to create; the nonbrilliant to experience brilliant breakthroughs; nonvisionaries to venture forth as if they know the future; and the execution-challenged to become "execution creatives" able to bring any reality into existence. As such, *Savanting* is a must-read for all aspiring worldbuilders and those committed to significant lifework.

As the name suggests, savanting is a savant-inspired protocol. In their field of genius, savants can surpass the performance of even the most intelligent among us. Yet they manage their amazing feats despite a damaged or deficient left brain which should make them incapable of such genius. In other words, *they outperform their potential.*

Savants prove that our brains have capabilities which most of us have never accessed. For years, scientists have tried unsuccessfully to unlock savant genius for all of us. While examining the latest research in savants, I had an epiphany. I suddenly surmised that savant genius was externally sourced. This would mean that it could be accessed by everyone. This does indeed seem to be the case.

Mine was not an out-of-the-blue epiphany. It was not as much of a stretch as one might assume. Since the early 90's, I had been investigating an internal-external partnership between the biological "machinery" within us dedicated to keeping us operating at our maximum and that same biological maximizing "machinery" acting on us from the outside which has evolved to maximize all living systems for survival.

In other words, I was investigating how to conscript the forces behind evolution to achieve significant goals more quickly. I have named these forces which maximize and advance all living systems in synergy and synchrony *the bioflow*.

What I discovered is that when we move towards our maximum operation, the internal and external maximizing "machineries" merge to become one. We experience a surge in our performance as if gears have engaged. The internal and external have obviously co-evolved to work together. What I seemed to have discovered was true human potential. A human potential which extended beyond the confines of our skin.

My challenge then became how to predictably engage this superachieving state sustainably and exploit it for more profound actualization and achievement. This intent has spawned the achievement technology called *savanting*.

I have re-integrated many people into the bio-infrastructure that adapts, evolves, and maximizes us for survival. By extending their capabilities with adaptive biological mechanisms, processes, and systems, they too can achieve beyond their innate potential as savants do.

The savanting strategies and modus operandi emerged from experimenting with and researching what I had learned from interviewing over 300 accomplished change executives from global multinationals in a compressed period of time. What I observed was then filtered through the lens of my degree in biological anthropology and my subsequent specialization in career and talent maximization.

Accordingly, all my books – fiction and nonfiction – explore the new level of human potential possible through re-integration into the evolutionary bio-machinery of which we are a subset and with which we have co-evolved to operate. Savanting is thus part of a larger body of work outlined below.

THE PRIMER

Peak Evolution: Beyond Peak Performance and Peak Experience (2001, 2010) was my first pass at trying to identify how to conscript this bio-infrastructure to experience evolved states, rapid growth, and a new level of peak performance in order to accelerate and amplify achievement.

APPLYING SAVANTING

BioMaxed (2019) is a collection of articles I wrote in 2013 and 2014 as I re-examined some of the latest scientific findings relevant to my research and consolidated what I had learned or developed since *Peak Evolution* was published in 2001.

The epiphany from savant research that is revealed in *Savanting* was captured in my 2013 article called *The New Career Maximums I* and included in the *BioMaxed* collection.

The articles in *BioMaxed* transition from the scientific research and analysis for reinforcing the protocol to its application to career-related matters. *Appendix III* is an excerpt from *BioMaxed* to help those wishing to quickly reset to their maximum in order to partner with the bioflow.

Learn how to exploit the bioflow from *fictional* characters

The Encore: A Transformational Thriller (2018) was an exciting opportunity to see savanting in action through *fictional* characters becoming heroic worldbuilders to save a planet. They comprise the supporting cast of the book's real main character, transformation.

The Encore lets you see how the bioflow operates and how it might be exploited to attain your goals. It is a visionary science-fiction ecothriller. The book is a hybrid of fiction and nonfiction in order to present my transformational savant-inspired protocol to those who do not read nonfiction. *The Encore* is the first book in a planned transformational novel series.

I have attached two excerpts from *The Encore* in appendices at the end of *Savanting* to provide additional information to help those who want to start to use savanting to harness evolutionary forces to assist in achieving significant, meaningful goals and contributions to the world.

Appendix I overviews savanting, the savant-inspired protocol. *Appendix II* will help you to more quickly discover your savant formula and how to define your savant domain where your genius will emerge.

Learn how to exploit the bioflow from successful _real_ people
Savanting: *Outperforming your Potential* (2019) is a chance to look at savanting in action in the lives of *real* people. First, the savants for which savanting is named are introduced and analyzed. I then examine whether savanting explains the success of the careers of some rather well-known superachievers – entrepreneurial CEOs Bill Gates, Steve Jobs, Jeff Bezos, Mark Zuckerberg, and Oprah plus entertainer Jim Carrey.

Thank you to these successful icons for lending us their very successful lives for study. We have much to learn from them about exploiting one's biological predisposition and the bioflow for one's greatest lifetime legacy.

Imagine a life filled with breakthroughs, flashes of genius, spontaneous knowledge events, and coincidences catapulting you to your goals faster. You are about to learn how to augment your creativity, inventiveness, and ingenuity to make your most meaningful impact on the world.

You'll also learn how to harness the evolutionary flow of humanity as a new directional guidance system by which to pilot your life and your work to maximum impact and advantage. This guidance system will keep you moving in the ideal direction for your growth and your goals. There is no greater strategic advantage for product developers or worldbuilders than to be compliant with the forefront of the evolutionary path of humanity and our world.

Above all, you are about to learn how to achieve beyond your internal potential. With a simple conversion to the unprecedented savanting modus operandi, true internal-external human potential can be released. The new savant-inspired protocol may allow you to surpass even the superlatives of savants. Prepare to transcend! The bar on human potential has been raised. You won't want to be left behind.

DID THESE ICONS SUCCEED WITH SAVANTING?

JIM CARREY	comedian, entertainer, actor, impressionist, screenwriter, film producer
OPRAH	media mogul, talk show host, actress, producer, philanthropist
STEVE JOBS	co-founder of Apple, information technology entrepreneur, inventor, a pioneer of the microcomputer revolution, Pixar computer-animation pioneer
BILL GATES	co-founder of Microsoft, information technology entrepreneur, mega-philanthropist pioneer, computer programmer, a pioneer of the microcomputer revolution
JEFF BEZOS	founder of Amazon.com, business leader, entrepreneur, e-commerce pioneer, aerospace pioneer
MARK ZUCKERBERG	co-founder of Facebook, internet entrepreneur, social networking pioneer, philanthropist

I

THE SAVANTS

Chapters

1

Externally Sourced Savantism

*Talent hits a target no one else can hit. Genius hits a
target no one else can see.*   Arthur Schopenhauer

The world's most famous savant, and certainly the most
beloved, is the fictional Raymond Babbitt. Dustin Hoffman
brilliantly portrayed the high-functioning autistic savant in
Rain Man, winner of *Best Picture* in 1988. Lightening quick
mathematical calculations. Encyclopedic recitations. Flawless
musical recitals or artwork replications after only one exposure.
Raymond was the first introduction for many to the breathtaking
feats of savants.

Savants outperform their potential. Science has yet to explain
the brilliance of savants. Their genius mysteriously exists despite
deficient left brains theoretically incapable of generating it.
Compelling arguments suggest that the superlatives of savants might
be externally sourced. This would mean that savant-level genius
could be accessible to us all. This is indeed the case.

Savanting is a breakthrough in human ingenuity, creativity,
and the actualization of one's true potential. It is an unprecedented
protocol formulated to unlock the potential of the human brain

already proven by savants. Yet it is simply a biology-based modus operandi to correct for interference by our cultures. It is a way to return to the way we were born to operate.

Achievements may be accelerated and amplified with this savant-inspired protocol. Noncreatives may deliver worldchanging creations, innovations, inventions and solutions. The nonbrilliant may experience brilliant breakthroughs. Nonvisionaries may venture forth to the forefront of human evolution as if they have envisioned the future.

The execution-challenged may become expeditious "execution creatives" able to bring even unknown frontiers into existence. In short, the ordinary may outperform even the savants to execute the extraordinary.

Savanting offers an entirely new way to attain some of man's most sought-after goals – extreme self-knowledge, self-love, wholeness, self-actualization, self-transcendence, nonduality, cosmic consciousness, and the revelation of one's biology-driven purpose.

Savanting engenders a sustainable state of peak-growth, peak-performance, peak-achievement, and peak-creation in the territory of your greatest talents and passion. It offers the guidance system so many seek to keep one on-path to one's greatest achievements, greatest purpose, greatest contribution, greatest meaning, and greatest rewards.

Because the savant-inspired protocol is biology-based, I suspect many of our most successful citizens have achieved that success from inadvertently operating as savanting prescribes. To prove this, I have provided analyses of the lives of some rather well-known superachievers – Bill Gates, Steve Jobs, Mark Zuckerberg, Jeff Bezos, Oprah Winfrey and Jim Carrey.

Was the savanting modus operandi their shared formula for success? You decide. To the extent that your answer is "Yes" you will have an opportunity to learn from the best how to use savanting to realize your full internal-external potential.

THE MYSTERY OF SAVANT INFORMATION ACCESS

The word "savant" comes from Middle French where it's the present participle of savoir, meaning "to know." The key factor behind savant superskills is their access to massive knowledge of both an encyclopedic and procedural nature. For example, this knowledge might include both how to play a musical instrument or a musical piece as well as a complete repertoire of music.

Savant encyclopedic information is usually narrowly confined to a particular subject. However, it is extraordinarily deep within the field of their genius. This massive information is never learned and the skills are never practiced. There is simply sudden knowledge.

This information access is the puzzle we must solve for us ordinary folk to fuel our own savant genius. In most cases savant brains are too damaged to either absorb or retain so much information. Theoretically they should not be able to do what they do. Mysteriously, decades of scientific research have not been able to identify where this information is stored within damaged savant brains.

Wilder Penfield (1891-1976), the celebrated Canadian-American neurosurgeon, mapped human brain function. He accomplished this by stimulating various areas of the brain with small electrical impulses while patients were awake during brain surgery. This process triggered patients to suddenly retrieve memories, see flashes of light, or smell an odor thus revealing the function of that area of the brain.

Stimulation of the temporal lobes often incited vivid recollections. This was proof of the physical basis of memory.[1] However, no such recall events have been provoked in savants.

Consequently, there appears to be no scientific evidence to dispute my hypothesis that savant genius could be sourced from the outside and is thus accessible to us all.

Externally sourced savantism would clear up a few longstanding mysteries about savants. Obviously, access to external information would finally explain why those with brains unable to absorb or retain information might nevertheless spout massive amounts of encyclopedic information. Each savant could be merely the conduit for an "external hard drive" from which information is streamed.

External sourcing would also explain why savant genius is normally limited to only one field. It would be logical to assume that at least some of the capabilities behind their single-field genius should spill over into other areas of the savant's life. It rarely does. *If savants have seemingly memorized massive amounts of data in their singular field of genius, why is this ability to memorize and retain information not transferrable to other fields?*

Access to external information would also explain why some savants do not even have to be exposed to the information to suddenly know it. The information is not in their memories. It never entered through their five senses. They never learned it. Rather, they are able to tap into an information constellation externally as and when they wish.

Yet there is more. Another savant mystery could be solved by my hypothesis. External information access could explain the spontaneous knowledge and skills of acquired savantism. In this syndrome, those of normal intelligence become instant savants when they suffer left-brain trauma such as a blow to the head, a cerebral insult from a stroke, being struck by lightning, or suffering dementia.

Artistic brilliance, mathematical mastery, photographic memory, and such may suddenly emerge. But here is the mystery.

Why do they suddenly possess fully formed, unlearned, savant superskills which were not in evidence prior to their injury?

Information and savantism are obviously intimately linked. This suggests an increased potential for all of us. We simply need the superior access to information that savants demonstrate. Logic dictates that if one group of human beings is capable of this superior access then we all are. Helping you to acquire this seemingly superhuman information sourcing skill is a major thrust of savanting.

SAVANT DOMAINS or FIELDS OF GENIUS

A closer examination of savant information access may reveal more clues. Raymond Babbitt is a composite of the attributes of multiple savants. This treasured fictional character has a larger range of skills or fields of expertise than most savants. This gives us an opportunity to learn more about the amazing capabilities of savants.

However, I must reveal two truths about savants which I suspect will help us nonsavants to replicate savant results. First, unlike Raymond, savants usually have mental abilities in only one specialized field. In this *"savant domain,"* their skills are superior to those of even the most intelligent human beings. Second, there are only five mainstream fields for savant genius. These are music, art, calendar recall, mathematics, and mechanical/visual-spatial skills.

If the savant domain is music, *a musical savant* could exhibit various forms of music-related brilliance. For example, they might be able to perform an entire piece of music flawlessly after hearing it only once. Or they might be able to play an instrument perfectly with no instruction. Or they might have an extensive repertoire of songs or pieces, any or all of which they may never have heard before.

Calendrical savants can quickly identify the day of the week, the weather, and events for any past calendar date. Calendar recall is another savant mystery. Why is this obscure skill almost universally present in savants? This encyclopedic information is simply known without learning or study by damaged savant brains incapable of absorbing, retaining, or calculating it.

If their savant domain is mathematics, *mathematical savants* may be able to complete what appears to be rapid, complex calculations and equations in their heads in seconds. They can arrive at these solutions even though most are incapable of even simple arithmetic.

You will learn from the accounts of one high-functioning savant, Daniel Tammet, that the mathematical solutions might not result from calculations at all but are yet another example of external access to encyclopedic information.

Savants whose domain forms around *mechanical/visual-spatial skills* may demonstrate very precise spatial location abilities and time-keeping skills without the need for a clock or other instruments. For example, they might be able to identify distances precisely without the benefit of measuring implements. Or they may be able to construct complex models or structures with painstaking accuracy. Or they might have mastered mapmaking and direction-finding.

Accessing "books" or systems of information

It appeared to me as if each savant had checked out only one "procedures manual" or one "system of information" from the library or database that defines the human species. The manual was for only one of the mainstream savant domains – for music or art or mathematics, for example. The manual's information is ordered, synergistic, and in-depth in that one field.

From this observation, there are two findings that reinforce my "external-sourcing" hypothesis. First, a savant's knowledge or intelligence is never elevated beyond the content of that procedural or activity manual. There is little new learning. And second, *all savants specializing in a specific savant domain seemed to access the same manual or system of information.* How else can one explain multiple savants having access to precisely the same information and skill?

SPECULATION ON SAVANT INFORMATION SOURCES

In his book, "Evolution's End: Claiming the Potential of Our Intelligence" (1992), developmental psychologist Joseph Chilton Pearce claims emphatically that "savants are untrained and untrainable, illiterate and uneducable . . . few can read or write . . . Yet each has apparently unlimited access to a particular field of knowledge that we know they cannot have acquired."[2]

Pearce reiterates for clarity: "The issue with these savants is that, in most cases, so far as can be observed, the savant has not acquired, could not have acquired, and is quite incapable of acquiring, the information that he so liberally dispenses."[3] This augurs well for my hypothesis of externally sourced savant genius and the information access behind it.

Dr. Darold A. Treffert was a clinical professor of psychiatry at the University of Wisconsin School of Medicine. He has studied savants since 1962 and continues at the Treffert Center in Fond du Lac, Wisconsin. As a renowned expert in savants, Treffert was the consultant recruited to advise on the "Rain Man" movie which introduced savants to the masses.

In his book, "Extraordinary People: Understanding Savant Syndrome" (2006), Dr. Treffert reveals, "Prodigious savants particularly "know" things, or "remember" things, they never learned."

He describes one savant whose conversational vocabulary was limited to some 58 words. Yet this savant could accurately identify the population of every city and town in the United States with more than 5,000 people; the names, number of rooms, and locations of 2,000 leading hotels in America; the distance from any city or town to the largest city in its state; statistics concerning 3,000 mountains and rivers; and the dates and essential facts of over 2,000 leading inventions and discoveries[4].

Dr. Treffert speculates that "certain persons, after head injury or disease, show explosive and sometimes prodigious musical, art, or mathematical ability, which lies dormant until released by a process of recruitment of still intact and uninjured brain areas, rewiring to those newly recruited areas and releasing the [until-then-latent-capacity] contained therein."[5]

That was 2006. By 2015, Dr. Treffert began to speculate that "genetic memory" is the source of the factual and procedural information behind savant genius. "Genetic memory, simply put, is complex abilities and actual sophisticated knowledge inherited along with other more typical and commonly accepted physical and behavioral characteristics. In savants the music, art or mathematical 'chip' comes factory installed."[6]

Both savant experts, Pearce and Treffert, and many more speculate on how savants might have this information. Yet there is no consensus and no provable conclusion. And, more importantly to our quest, there is no means yet identified for those of normal intelligence to replicate the information access of savant genius.

So, when I propose externally sourced savantism, there is no scientific alternative and no scientific evidence to disprove my hypothesis. However, if the savanting methodology presented in this book works to increasingly give you more access to spontaneous information in your savant domain, you will have your own proof – the only proof that counts.

To the speculation on genetic memory as the explanation for savant information access, I would have to question or comment as follows:

- Why do the memory and savant skills not spread outside of the savant's field of genius or savant domain?
- Why are there so few savant domains in the genes of the entire human race?
- Why, after decades of research, have so many gifted scientists not been able to locate the mechanisms of this internal information storage in savant brains or genes?
- Why have most of us never experienced evidence that we contain massive amounts of information which we have not assimilated through our five senses?
- In addition, the information accessed by savants is too specific to a savant domain to be selected by evolution to be engrained in the DNA of our entire species. What evolutionary challenge could possibly have invoked a DNA adaptation to music, mathematics, or calendrical data? It benefits neither the survival of the individual nor the species.
- Further, imagine how big our memory storage in our brains or genes would have to be if we each had to keep our own copy of even just the encyclopedic information of each savant domain.
- How would current information be continually updated? Think of calendrical savants, for example. Or what about the example of the savant Treffert described who knows all the populations of every city and town in the United States? This is evolving information. The information is too current to have been encoded in our DNA or in that savant's head prior to his injury. If something were to be encoded, it would more likely be the means to stimulate the inflow of the externally sourced information behind savant superskills.

- As we know from the information technology field, it would be a nightmare to keep the copy of the database in each of us up to date. Evolution would have favored instead the simplicity of having a single copy of the information and ensuring each of us had the means to access it.

This is exactly what I think evolution did since the savanting modus operandi we are investigating reveals the means to access it. Genetic memory is neither proven nor logical in the case of either savants or nonsavants so it doesn't argue against my external-sourcing hypothesis.

> *Savant syndrome and autism, I think, are not disorders of brain structure, but they're disorders of brain function.*   Dr. Darold A. Treffert

---

[1]   Wilder Penfield, *The Mystery of Mind.* Princeton: Princeton University Press; 1975; and
The Montreal procedure: The legacy of the great Wilder Penfield,
Lady Diana Ladinoa, Syed Rizvib, José Francisco Téllez-Zentenob
April 26, 2018, https://doi.org/10.1016/j.yebeh.2018.04.001
[2]   Joseph Chilton Pearce, *Evolution's End . In: San Francisco, CA: HarperSanFrancisco; 1992;p. 3-5*
[3]   Joseph Chilton Pearce *Evolution's End . In: San Francisco, CA: HarperSanFrancisco; 1992;p. 3-5*
[4]   Darold A.Treffert, *Extraordinary People: Understanding Savant Syndrome .* In: Lincoln, NE: iUuniverse Inc; 2006;p. 396
[5]   Darold A.Treffert, *Genetic Memory: How We Know Things We Never Learned,* January 28, 2015, *Scientific American Guest Blog*
https://blogs.scientificamerican.com/guest-blog/genetic-memory-how-we-know-things-we-never-learned
[6]   Darold A.Treffert, *Genetic Memory,* January 28, 2015

2

Famous Savants

The lives of Bill Gates, Steve Jobs, Jeff Bezos, Mark Zuckerberg, Oprah and Jim Carrey are going to help us to identify a new modus operandi for operating at peak potential with savant-like genius. Before we begin this fascinating investigation, let's first explore savant genius in some of the world's best-known savants.

The Rain Man movie (1988) – a prodigious autistic savant

Dustin Hoffman's role as high-functioning savant Raymond Babbitt in the 1988 Best Picture, *Rain Man,* earned him Best Actor honors. Babbitt juxtaposes deficiencies in social interaction, language, and sensory processing with rare abilities in math and memory. He is a mental calculator with the ability to instantly count hundreds of objects at once.

In preparation, Hoffman spent many hours watching films of savants and meeting them in person. He was then in a position to animate Babbitt's composite savant character. The award-winning actor may owe much of the character to his time with Kim Peek due to Kim's rare megasavant status.

Kim Peek or "Kimputer" – a megasavant

"Kimputer" was born without the thick band of axons connecting his left- and right-brain hemispheres. Like Babbitt, Kim was capable of incredible feats of memory and math. He could recall over 12,000 books and had a nearly complete and up-to-date knowledge of world history, area codes, zip codes, roads and highways, and much more. No matter what date was given to him, Kim could describe the events of the day. Give him a location and Kim could identify the zip code. No wonder we all have savant envy.

Kim's astonishing abilities included being able to read one page of a book with his left eye and the other with his right. It took Kim just eight seconds to read and remember a page. Peek was classed as a megasavant because of his phenomenal knowledge in fifteen broad domains from history and literature and geography to numbers, sports, music, and dates. Kim is the exception in not having just one prevailing savant domain. His encyclopedic recitation of facts was legendary.

However, these breathtaking capabilities were in stark contrast to his severe mental handicaps and motor skill insufficiencies. Kim could not perform ordinary tasks such as getting dressed, combing his hair, or turning off the lights. He could not figure things out. He could only recite facts. Given his mental deficiencies, his source of these facts was likely external.

> *Someday you'll be as great as I am.*
> Kim Peek, Kimputer, a megasavant

Orlando Serrell – acquired or sudden-onset savantism

Orlando Serrell had no savant superskills until he received a brain injury at the age of ten. Orlando was hit hard on the left side of his head by a baseball. From then on, he discovered that he had acquired the calendar skills common to savants. He could perform complex calendar "calculations" and remember the weather every day from the day of the accident. Name a date and Orlando would tell you not only the day of the week but whether or not it was raining in the area where he resided. There was not even a hint of these skills before the accident.

Acquired savantism or *acquired savant syndrome* defines those of normal intelligence whose left brains have been severely damaged later in life through injury, dementia or illness. What is so fascinating is that their genius-level skills emerge spontaneously fully formed. Acquired savantism is by far the most promising aspect of savant study for augmenting human potential.

As with Daniel Tammet below, Orlando claims he does not calculate. He has not memorized calendars. Nor does he use complicated algorithms to arrive at his calendar-related feats. He says he can just see the answers in front of him.

Orlando thus is a confirmation of my external-information-access hypothesis. This seems more likely than the suggestion of some savant researchers that he is doing superhuman calendar calculations in a brain incapable of them.

And external sourcing also seems more likely than Orlando having the information in his memory. This is because (a) he never learned it and (b) his damaged brain is incapable of such memorization and (c) there was no evidence of that information prior to the injury thus ruling out genetic memory passed from generations and (d) because his information remains current and genetic memory could not explain that.

Stephen Wiltshire – the human camera

As an autistic savant, Stephen Wiltshire also has an exceptional if not superhuman talent. Stephen is an artist who draws and paints detailed cityscapes. Wiltshire originals sell for thousands of pounds. Stephen demonstrated his genius at an early age. By age eight, he received his first commission. It was from the British Prime Minister who asked that he create a drawing of Salisbury Cathedral.

Stephen can draw an accurate and detailed landscape of a city after seeing it just once! Wiltshire drew a ten-meter long panorama of Tokyo following a short helicopter ride. It took Stephen only eight days to complete the artwork using a pen.

So the question to ask yourself is, "Is it more likely that Wiltshire accessed the detailed images from an external information database or from his memory?" Consider that he only glimpsed the city briefly. Could Stephen have seen enough detail in a brief pass in the helicopter to capture and record the information in his memory? It seems more likely that he had ongoing access to the details externally.

Daniel Tammet – a prodigious autistic savant with Asperger's syndrome

Daniel is an impressive high-functioning autistic savant. There are fewer than 100 known *prodigious savants* alive and Daniel is one of them. This means his abilities would be exceptional even if he didn't have disabilities. Tammet is a paradox of both extraordinary ability and disability. He can't do the simplest of tasks.

Yet Daniel Tammet is a mathematical and linguistic genius. He is a *polyglot savant* with multi-language fluency. He speaks eleven languages – one of which he learned in a week for a TV special. As a proven expert, he has described a new way for learning new languages. He is known for incredible feats of memorization and mental "calculation" similar to those of Raymond Babbitt. He recited the number pi up to the 22,514th digit thus breaking the European record.

Insight into savantism

Tammet is important to our current pursuit of savantism for those with normal intelligence because he is articulate enough to provide unprecedented insight into how savants operate. He can also explain autism and offer hope for its treatment.

Professor Allan Snyder from the Centre for the Mind at the Australian National University in Canberra explains why Tammet is of scientific interest. "Savants can't usually tell us how they do what they do. It just comes to them. Daniel can. He describes what he sees in his head. That's why he's exciting. He could be the Rosetta Stone."[7]

Many savants struggle with language and comprehension – skills associated primarily with the left-brain hemisphere. They often have amazing skills in mathematics and memory because these are primarily right-hemisphere skills. Typically, savants have a limited vocabulary, but this is not the case with Tammet. He has the ability to think abstractly, to deviate from routine, and to empathize, interact, and communicate with others.

Daniel describes how he accomplishes his amazing feats in his memoir, the award-winning New York Times bestseller "Born on a Blue Day: Inside the Extraordinary Mind of an Autistic Savant" (2007). It has been translated into 24 languages. He is also the author of the international bestsellers "Embracing the Wide Sky: A Tour across the Horizons of the Mind" (2009) and "Thinking in Numbers: On Life, Love, Meaning, and Math" (2014).

Mathematical solutions without calculations

I think you can see why I might conclude that Daniel's languages and memorization skills could be the result of accessing information from an "external hard drive." However, as I alluded in the previous chapter, his seeming calculations turn out to not be calculations at all. Rather they represent the same access to external data I am surmising for all savants and thus for those of normal intelligence aspiring to savant genius.

Daniel can provide the solution to the multiplication of enormous sums effortlessly in seconds with the speed and accuracy of a computer. In fact, he can determine cube roots faster than any calculator. Tammet has explained different ways of "knowing" mathematical solutions without linear calculations. There is a youtube.com video of Daniel instructing on his very uncalculating ways of arriving at answers which will surprise you.[8]

"When I multiply numbers together, I see two shapes," explains Tammet. "The image starts to change and evolve, and a third shape emerges. That's the answer. It's mental imagery. It's like math without having to think."[9] *It is not a conscious act at all.* He sees numbers as shapes, colors and textures.

Daniel calls it "mathematics without thinking" for a reason. Tammet sees each number up to 10,000 as a different shape, pattern, color, personality, mood, and/or emotion. The number two, for example, is a motion, and five is a clap of thunder. If he wants to multiply two numbers, the images he associates with each combine in his mind to produce a new shape which he instantly recognizes as the correct number.

Thus, Daniel arrives at his "computation" answers via mental images rather than calculating – *mental images which might reflect the access to an external database through Tammet's synesthesia.* Synesthesia is the production of a sense impression relating to one sense or part of the body by stimulation of another sense or part of the body, He *experiences* the mathematical solutions rather than *calculates* them.

External Access

I alluded to "thinking in pictures" for the "photographic mind" of the human camera, Stephen Wiltshire. Isn't it interesting that with Tammet we have another savant with different skills who also arrives at his brilliant outcomes through pictures? Pictures offer a short form for communicating massive amounts of information. Perhaps other savants are also receiving the massive information behind their superskills via pictures.

The award-winning biopic, "Temple Grandin," was about an autistic savant who became one of the top scientists in the humane livestock handling industry. Temple Grandin is also the author of "Thinking in Pictures." She too reveals she sources the information behind her savant superskills through pictures. "My mind works like Google for images. You put in a key word; it brings up pictures."

However, I've buried the lead. In one of the strongest twists in favor of my hypothesis, Tammet apparently has physical damage in the regions of the brain in which calculations are done. This explains why Daniel cannot do algebra. One would expect that he could do these kinds of calculations if he was indeed the wizard at mathematical calculations that he appears to be.

Here is another hypothesis. One could imagine mathematical answers as already existing in the external database and Daniel is simply accessing them. His synesthesia may be an unnecessary twist to his data access for those wishing to replicate his genius. This would make his external sourcing of information much like the encyclopedic access of all other savants. This continues to reinforce the idea that savant-like genius could be available to all of us if we simply discovered the means to link to the external database.

Passion for one's savant domain

"I do love numbers," Daniel shares. "It isn't only an intellectual or aloof thing that I do. I really feel that there is an emotional attachment, a caring for numbers. I think this is a human thing – in the same way that a poet humanises a river or a tree through metaphor, my world gives me a sense of numbers as personal. It sounds silly, but numbers are my friends."[10]

Daniel's passion for his savant domain is evident. This passion for the work in one's savant domain is consistent with the experience of nonsavants in their field of genius as prescribed by savanting. The lives of Bill Gates, Steve Jobs, Jeff Bezos, Mark Zuckerberg, Oprah and Jim Carrey will demonstrate this same passion for the intrinsically rewarding work in their own savant domains.

Daniel helps us to see this crossover. Savanting is a savant-inspired protocol. A simple behavioral change to a savant modus operandi may enable our own access to their genius.

Daniel Tammet Quotes

- *In my mind, numbers and words are far more than squiggles of ink on a page. They have form, color, texture and so on. They come alive to me, which is why as a young child I thought of them as my "friends."*

- *37 is a lumpy number, a bit like porridge. Six is very small and dark and cold, and whenever I was little trying to understand what sadness is I would imagine myself inside a number six and having that experience of cold and darkness. Similarly, number four is a shy number.*

- *I would play with numbers in a way that other kids would play with their friends.*

- *I recited Pi to 22,514 decimal points in five hours and nine minutes. I was able to do this because of weeks of study, aided by the unusual synaesthesic way my mind perceives numbers as complex multidimensional coloured and textured shapes.*

- *Squaring numbers is a symmetrical process that I like very much. And when I divide one number by another, say, 13 divided by 97, I see a spiral rotating downwards in larger and larger loops that seem to warp and curve. The shapes coalesce into the right number. I never write anything down.*

---

[7]   Richard Johnson, *A Genius Explains*, interview with savant Daniel Tammet, February 12, 2005, The Guardian
http://www.theguardian.com/theguardian/2005/feb/12/weekend7.weekend2
[8]   Daniel Tammet, *Autistic savant Daniel Tammet on 'the language of numbers*,' August 23, 2017, BBC Newsnight,
https://www.youtube.com/watch?v=j3Mecg8iuuE
[9]   Richard Johnson, *A Genius Explains*
[10]   Richard Johnson, *A Genius Explains*

II

SAVANT-LIKE

Chapters

3

The Savant Domains of NonSavants

You are about to learn the secret to savanting and savant genius. Finally, the missing methodology for savant-level information access will be revealed. Here is the key. *Nonsavants also have a specific savant domain in which genius occurs.* This domain is also biologically determined as it is in savants.

Magic happens when we apply our strongest, most rewarding talents to the most meaningful, intrinsically rewarding tasks which stretch us beyond our previous capabilities. This is the formula for operating at our biological maximum. In this peak state, our left brains are rewired to shut off the gatekeeper which is selectively filtering the information which continually bombards our awareness.

As with savants, domain-specific encyclopedic and procedural information is free to flow in. Or, more precisely for nonsavants, information relevant to our savant-domain activity becomes available to our awareness. Creativity is the re-combining of existing information systems to generate a novel information system. Therefore, with greater information inflow, our creativity and creations will increase.

Renowned American cognitive psychologist, Howard Gardner, reinforces the genius possible in one's savant domain:

"All creative work occurs in one or more domains. Individuals are not creative (or noncreative) in general; they are creative in particular domains of accomplishment and require the achievement of expertise in these domains before they can execute significant creative work."[11]

Other researchers have also commented on the relationship between creative talent and domain expertise: Amabile, Phillips, & Collins (1994),[12] for example. However, here is where savanting advances the findings of the established experts.

In my experience, the above formula for operating at our biological maximum defines a singular savant domain in which the greatest creativity, breakthroughs, and genius occurs. It is the domain for which each individual is most biologically predisposed.

It is tricky to define one's savant domain because it may or may not coincide with an existing field or discipline. This is why I believe psychologist Howard Gardner gave himself some wiggle room in allowing more than one domain.

However, savanting offers a biology-based approach which has more precision. This domain of peak performance, peak potential, and savant-like genius may be identified by biological events internally and externally. More about the identification of one's savant domain shortly.

Bioflow

The *bioflow* is what I have named the forces behind evolution. These are the forces which maximize and advance all living systems in synergy and synchrony. This includes the maximizing of the human species and each of us. It is what I call the external maximizing machinery.

When one does meaningful work at our biological maximum by applying our strongest, most rewarding talents, a biological transformation occurs. One experiences a surge into a biological overdrive state.

Our internal maximizing machinery – all the systems keeping our body operating in top form – re-links with the bioflow's external maximizing machinery with which we have co-evolved to operate. In fact, it appears that there is not an internal and external system at all but instead a singular biological maximizing system.

There is evidence that preschoolers are still connected to the bioflow. Our cultures have mistakenly taught us to operate as separate entities when, in fact, we are born fully integrated into the dynamics of the biological infrastructure around us. True human potential then obviously has both an internal and external component.

Damaged savant brains are unable to absorb the rules of culture. Savants therefore never learned how to separate from the bio-machinery into which we are all born. I believe the six superachievers we will be examining – Bill Gates, Steve Jobs, Jeff Bezos, Mark Zuckerberg, Oprah and Jim Carrey – also did not separate from the bioflow or did so only briefly during their lives.

To attain savant genius, then, we need only to restore our integration into the bioflow. This will complete circuits and engage gears – physically, biologically, biochemically and electromagnetically – which evolution has painstakingly evolved to work together. Only then will we know the full potential of humanity.

Savantflow

What is our maximum? It occurs when one shifts biologically to an altered state of consciousness during what I call *savantflow – our savant-domain flow state*. This is a specialized subset of the peak-performance flow states that Csikszentmihalyi introduced in his breakthrough book, *Flow: The Psychology of Optimal Experience* (1990).[13]

Csikszentmihalyi identifies flow as "a state in which people are so involved in an activity that nothing else seems to matter; the experience is so enjoyable that people will continue to do it even at great cost, for the sheer sake of doing it."

He further notes, "Contrary to what we usually believe . . . the best moments in our lives, are not the passive, receptive, relaxing times . . . The best moments usually occur when a person's body or mind is stretched to its limits in a voluntary effort to accomplish something difficult and worthwhile. Optimal experience [(flow)] is thus something that we make happen."[14]

Flow is a state of such fusion with the task at hand that everything else – including self-awareness – disappears. It is an altered state of consciousness which may deepen over time to come to rival the aesthetic rapture of artists and musicians or even the ecstasy of religious mystics.

Athletes label flow as "being in the zone." In fact, flow is so critical to their peak performance that flow coaches are hired to ensure they can engage that state during their competitive events. Research shows that flow states induce exponential growth in performance, meaning, learning, creativity, motivation, willpower, pattern recognition and lateral thinking.

Savantflow is the specialized flow state that emerges when you are applying your strongest, most rewarding constellation of talents, strengths, and skills to your most meaningful and engaging work for the most valuing audience – real or imagined. As such, savantflow is an action-oriented, creative state not a passive, meditative one.

It is this state of consciousness during activity fusion which disarms the left-brain gatekeeper to allow the inflow of information that savants experience. The difference is that savants seem to download the whole "book" for their savant domain, while nonsavants download only the information relevant to the activity which is generating their savantflow.

It appears that the damaged brains of savants and the savantflow brains of nonsavants operating in their savant domain both yield the information access behind savant-like genius.

Savantflow is one of many mechanisms we have evolved to entice us to operate at our biological maximum. It is our means to effortlessly merge with the bioflow to shift us into overdrive. It therefore engages a constellation of irresistible drives and emotional highs to ensure we continuously want to return to this wondrous state.

Consequently, savantflow is an addictive state. Evolution undoubtedly determined that having a multitude of attractors to keep us operating at our maximum would offer the individual and the species the best chance of survival.

In normal flow states, all the resources of one's brain and body are recruited to perform the task at hand. One is thus performing at one's peak. Savantflow goes one step beyond. It also recruits the power, resources, capabilities, and living and information systems of the bioflow relevant to the savant-domain activity which has incited one's flow state.

Serial savantflows reveal one's savant domain

Savantflows emerge from applying your strongest, most rewarding talents to the most meaningful work to which you are passionately drawn for an audience that would value that work. The work that can incite your savantflows – and thus your re-integration into the bioflow – defines your savant domain.

Serial savantflows as a way of life are the underlying dynamic driving savanting, the savant-inspired protocol. Their progressive advance and deepening are what will come to define your savant domain.

In the beginning you may only perceive a familiar exhilarating state of being as your savant domain. You may not have epithets with which to label it. It may take a history of savantflow events before you discover the theme and can identify words to define your savant domain. It may not be an existing field or discipline of study. Rather, it is the field of genius which gives voice to your unique creative expression.

Your domain-specific savant formula

Savanting's target state of being for experiencing savant-level genius is serial savantflows within one's savant domain within the bioflow. Your personal savant formula then will tell you how to achieve the desired partnership with the bioflow. Figuring this out is easier than you might think.

Past bioflow support predicts future bioflow support. This is because the biological maximum of your system is a constant and the way the bioflow pressures your system to maximize is also a constant. Your personal formula then can be identified by whatever pattern or theme of activities in your past has provoked serial savantflows within your savant domain within the bioflow.

There are two key indicators of past bioflow support. First, you'll want to identify the theme of the activities which have caused internal spontaneous information events such as breakthroughs, flashes of genius, epiphanies, and creative inspirations.

Second, you'll want to identify when external spontaneous information events emerged which accelerated your progress. These are events in your reality such as clusters of coincidences, models, and facilitating people and events.

These are all information leaps. Because the internal and external maximizing mechanisms belong to the same maximizing machinery, savant-domain activities which generate leaps internally will also generate them externally. I have divided them for convenience for this exercise, but they are part of the same information support process for your creativity and creations in savantflow.

This brings us to the obvious third theme of activities that you'll want to investigate – those activities which caused you to enter savantflow. All three of these patterns of activities are most likely to occur in bulk when you are working in your savant domain.

Only rarely will these patterns emerge in other fields of endeavor. This simple inventory of past events will enable you to identify the themes for what will cause bioflow support in your future. As promised, you now have a biology-based approach for identifying your savant domain.

Notice that either your *savantflows theme* or your *sudden-knowledge theme* will identify the same savant formula. They are interchangeable. Therefore, you can pick the one that is easiest for you when you are trying to determine your savant formula or when you are trying to make ongoing decisions in the future to sustain bioflow support.

Here's what I said in my *Sourcing your Savant* chapters in *BioMaxed* (2019),[15] "You can capitalize on this consistency and predictability. You can predict the future from your past. Imagine knowing in advance that a project will succeed or fail. Predictability enables project and goal selections which will have a greater chance of success.

"As a corollary, it also means you will not be damaged by choosing projects that will be opposed by the maximizing bioflow. Let's begin now to examine historically the circumstances around your past peak performances and breakthroughs. We may then develop a savant formula to repeat, accelerate, and amplify exceptional performance in your future."

I go into detail on how to determine your savant formula in these same *Sourcing your Savant* chapters in *BioMaxed* for those who need more information on how to make the paradigm shift to savanting.

To supplement this source, I have included an excerpt from *The Encore: A Transformational Thriller* (2018) in "Appendix I" of this book which overviews savanting and its potential impact. Appendix II holds another excerpt from *The Encore* which will assist those ready to discover their savant domain and begin applying the savant-inspired protocol to their goals.

I want to mention a few more patterns of events that you may wish to examine in your past to help you to better navigate in the future to sustain your bioflow connection. They will also enable you to better assess the application of savanting in the lives of Bill Gates, Steve Jobs, Jeff Bezos, Mark Zuckerberg, Oprah and Jim Carrey.

First, examine past events for your *unpaid work theme*. This is work for which others would charge but which you crave so much that you'd do it for free. This work is the creative expression of the essence of your system. It causes your genius to surface. Its where you are continuously impressed with your amazing performance.

You could also look at past patterns of events associated with your *knowledge-pursuit* or *learning-pursuit* or *growth-pursuit theme*. What is the theme of the knowledge you have craved in the past? Think of the times when you exerted great effort to find out new information. What was the field? Could it be related to work you crave doing? It is likely that you'll find that you've been seeking knowledge passionately and willingly for the application and improvement of your strongest most rewarding talents.

Next, you'll want to determine your *frontier-pursuit theme*. What are the new frontiers of growth, learning and achievement which you have been drawn to pursue even though you are normally resistant to penetrating unknown territories? Again, the frontiers pursued are likely to relate to the application of your key talents for meaningful causes because this is what will maximize your system.

Most of us are fearful of venturing into the unknown. However, you'll be surprised to discover that there will be at least one generic territory where you are not only less fearful of the unknown but you are exhilarated by it. This will be your savant domain.

Also look for your *creativity-pursuit theme*. What do the patterns of past events tell you about your preferences for creativity, invention, innovation and other ways in which you change reality with the new and unprecedented.

An examination of past events for your *meaning-pursuit theme* will indicate the type of work or achievements or contributions that you consider a meaningful application of key talents.

All these themes plus your *spontaneous-knowledge theme* and your *savantflows theme* will be sending you in the same direction – biological maximization – just as you would expect from evolution's dedication to our survival.

Therefore, they may be used interchangeably for determining your savant formula. More importantly, they will serve as a guide for ongoing directional decision-making in the future so you may sustain support from the bioflow.

Over time, serial savantflows will define an ever deepening and evolving field of genius or savant domain where your peak performance and peak potential can accomplish your greatest lifework.

Most men lead lives of quiet desperation and go to
the grave with the song still in them.
Henry David Thoreau

---

[11] Howard Gardner (1993). *Creating Minds.* New York: Basic Books, p. 145

[12] Amabile, T. M., E. Phillips, and M. A. Collins. "Person and Environment in Talent Development: The Case of Creativity." In *Talent Development: Proceedings of the 1993 Henry B. and Jocelyn Wallace National Research Symposium on Talent Development*, edited by Nicholas Colangelo, Susan G. Assouline, and DeAnn L. Ambroson. Unionville, NY: Trillium Press, 1994. https://www.hbs.edu/faculty/Pages/item.aspx?num=1073

[13] Mihaly Csikszentmihalyi, *Flow: The Psychology of Optimal Experience* 1990, New York: Harper & Row

[14] Mihaly Csikszentmihalyi, *Flow: Psychology of Happiness*, 1992, Rider & Co

[15] Lauren Holmes, *BioMaxed* (2019), *Sourcing your Savant* chapters, p. 51-100

4

Savant Domains from Childhood

The six superachievers I have selected to demonstrate savanting have pursued what I consider biologically maximized careers – ones which honor their biological predispositions in compliance with the bioflow. One's biological wiring, one's strongest most rewarding talents, and one's savant domain are more obvious during the simplicity of childhood. Therefore, it would be enlightening to examine what preceded their illustrious careers.

In my view, these six successful models never left the internal-external maximizing machinery into which we are all born. They remained integrated into the bioflow for most of their careers. Accordingly, their capabilities were always extended by the external bio-infrastructure and informational databases.

They live(d) maximized lives of continuous savantflows within their savant domain. Not only were they operating from peak performance, but they were in a high-growth state which continually pushed the envelope on their baseline functionality and the advance of their savant domain. As a result of being guided by the bioflow – the evolutionary flow of all living systems – they each pioneered new frontiers for humanity.

The new savant-inspired mode of operation will be examined in the lives of the four iconic founders of Amazon, Microsoft, Apple, and Facebook – Jeff Bezos, Bill Gates, Steve Jobs, and Mark Zuckerberg, respectively. Excerpts from the lives of these and other superachievers will model how the internal-external partnership may be exploited to generate the worldchanging achievements they each attained.

"Control" of nature versus "compliance"

I have also selected the lives of two additional icons from very different savant domains as models. I specifically chose Oprah and Jim Carrey because they have self-identified as celebrity proponents of the law-of-attraction movement. I think you'll find that explaining their success is much easier through savanting than the law of attraction (LOA). Their success will certainly be more replicable with savanting.

I also chose Oprah and Carrey because there are publicized events in their lives which are instructional with respect to pursuing the savanting way of life. This is my purpose for having six models. In addition, I think you'll come to see that all their favorite success stories used to promote LOA result from honoring their biological wiring as savanting promotes.

In one critical way, the law of attraction is the exact opposite of savanting which is itself instructional. Savanting outlines a means *to comply with* internal and external biological processes in order to achieve goals associated with self-actualization and biology-driven purpose.

The law of attraction has the expectation of *controlling* natural forces. It is about *redirecting* natural forces to materialize what one wants through "like" attracting "like." I assume this means that theoretically everyone in the world can simultaneously change the direction of powerful integrated and co-dependent universal forces to attract money. A bit of a challenge to reasoned thinking.

Savanting is about biological maximization. Both Carrey and Oprah were true to their biological predisposition in advancing their savant domains. Their success was achieved through sustained self-actualization. Have a look at their lives in the coming chapters and decide for yourself whether they controlled or complied with natural forces.

For now, let's examine snapshots of the childhoods of all six superachievers for the beginnings of the savant domains in which they achieved such sensational success. I think the parallels of their biologically maximized careers will inspire your career.

THE CHILDHOODS OF OUR SIX SUPERACHIEVERS

Jim Carrey – *comedian, entertainer, actor, impressionist, screenwriter, film producer, **uplifter***

Jim Carrey was an entertainer from birth. He was addicted to uplifting people's spirits. As a young boy, Jim slept with his tap shoes on in case his parents needed cheering up during the night. Unfortunately, his father had become unemployed and their financial situation had become dire. Carrey applied to be on the Carol Burnett Show at age ten and gave his first standup comedy performance at a comedy club at age sixteen. The savant domain in which he ultimately became successful began in his childhood.

Oprah – *media mogul, talk show host, actress, producer, philanthropist, **uplifter***

When Oprah was just three and a half, she was passionate about preaching to help people. She loved to recite the uplifting sermons of renowned preachers in the churches around her home. She knew even then that she aspired to inspire, encourage, and uplift.

Her talent as an orator and storyteller and her gift for drawing out people's stories to benefit others were all in evidence by the age of five. She took drama in high school. During her senior year, WVOL, an African-American radio station in Nashville, Tennessee hired Oprah to read the news. Her broadcasting career was launched.

She then won a public speaking contest which gave her a scholarship to Tennessee State University. She majored in speech communications and performing arts. As with our other four founders, Oprah too left university in her teens to do the work she was passionate about. She accepted a job as a co-anchor at a CBS television station.

In 1978, while she was in her early twenties, Oprah was offered her first talk show to co-host, a morning show called "People are Talking." After her first show, Oprah knew that this is what she wanted to do for the rest of her life. The savant domain of her ultimate success began in her childhood.

Steve Jobs – *co-founder of Apple, information technology entrepreneur, **consumer engineer and artist**, inventor, microcomputer industry pioneer, Pixar computer-animation pioneer*

Steve Jobs was committed to consumer engineering for electronics from his early teens. That is the only audience that has ever connected to his heart. Jobs' mechanical prowess and passion began at an early age. By age ten, Steve's attraction to electronics had become obvious to his parents. As a result, he spent long hours with his father dismantling and rebuilding electronic devices in the family garage.

When he was twelve years old, he called William Hewlett, co-founder of Hewlett-Packard, to ask him for some parts to complete a school project. Impressed, Hewlett offered Jobs an internship at his company. Jobs thus launched into his savant domain before he was even a teenager.

Hewlett-Packard became a model for how he would run Apple at such a young age. Jobs and Apple co-founder Steve Wozniak met in high school when Jobs was just thirteen. Woz was the first person Jobs had met who knew more about electronics than he did. Their days quickly became about the type of work that eventually created Apple and made Jobs a leader in his savant domain.

Steve's entrepreneurial skills showed up early in his life with several commercializations with Woz while a teenager. His love for minimalist design used for all Apple products also started in his teens and is rooted in the modernist architecture of his childhood home and his study of the principles of simplicity in Japanese Zen Buddhism. He took art classes in his teens to develop his interest.

Bill Gates – *co-founder of Microsoft, information technology entrepreneur, mega-philanthropy pioneer, software pioneer, microcomputer industry pioneer,* **worldbuilder**

By the time Bill Gates was thirteen, his key talents had intersected into a savant domain focused on improving the quality of life of *individuals en masse*. Bill's brilliance in the tools of his mission – programming and business – were winning him acclaim and money throughout his teens.

In fact, he knew as a pre-teen that he would be an entrepreneur running his own company. However, his entrepreneurialism embraced the true meaning of the word with respect to pioneering new frontiers not simply business ownership.

Gates had a passion and aptitude for penetrating the unknown and building the structure to underpin it. The words of Ralph Waldo Emerson come to mind. "Do not go where the path may lead, go instead where there is no path and leave a trail."

These three talents – business, programming and entrepreneurialism – were only tools of Bill's worldbuilding domain. So many have missed the essence of the man and what drives him because they assumed (a) that the accouterments of success he accumulated from his achievements were his goal or (b) that the fields or industries in which he played identified his savant domain. Had Microsoft never existed, Bill Gates' career would have looked exactly the same in some other frontier.

He was ready to launch his first company by age fifteen but was overruled by his parents wanting him to attend university. By the time he was twenty his passions had found vent in Microsoft which launched two new fields – microcomputers and software – in the service of personal computing.

Microsoft let him begin his widespread service to enhancing the lives of consumers *en ma*sse until it was easier to do this more directly through philanthropy, or more precisely, mega-philanthropy. This had been a key focus of his family from his birth.

Jeff Bezos – *founder of Amazon.com, business leader, entrepreneur, e-commerce pioneer, aerospace pioneer,* ***worldbuilder***

Jeff Bezos is considered to be the inventor and developer of e-commerce through Amazon.com. Amazon has transformed the way we read, shop and watch TV, and through its cloud services division runs an astonishingly large portion of the internet.

Bezos is a self-proclaimed "change junkie" continuously scaling new frontiers of learning, experimentation, and creation. At age eighteen, Jeff's valedictorian speech at his high school revealed his vision of the retail and residential expansion of humanity into space. This colonization vision undoubtedly drove the planetary expansion of Amazon.

In addition, Jeff has now founded a consumer spaceflight company, Blue Origin, to develop the necessary technology for establishing an enduring human presence in space. Commercial suborbital human spaceflight experimentation began in 2018. The planet-wide expansion of Amazon into new unknown territories was preparation for the new frontiers he hopes to scale for the colonization of space.

The savant domain that spawned both Amazon and Blue Origin first appeared as Jeff's obsession with science fiction books emphasizing worldbuilding. Even as a child his mind was captivated by their ambitious, mogul-driven projects with a self-contained set of planets, space colonies, and social relations (human, post-human, or other-than-human) run by radically different principles from the ones we know.

Following an announcement ceremony for Blue Origin at Cape Canaveral, Bezos talked with the media about his childhood obsession with the space program and science fiction books, and how that passion has motivated his business pursuits and shaped his ultimate goal to eventually put "millions of people" into space.

While an undergraduate at Princeton, Bezos served as the President of Princeton's Students for the Exploration and Development of Space. His goal has always been to continuously make history. One can trace Bezos' savant domain from childhood to the present and even project it into the future. Even if Amazon disappeared from the world tomorrow, we can know where his life will go. He will be true to his biological wiring.

Mark Zuckerberg – *co-founder of Facebook, internet entrepreneur, social networking pioneer, philanthropist,* ***worldbonder***

According to his tutor in grade school, Mark Zuckerberg was a programming prodigy. Many assume this is his savant domain. However, Mark was smart at everything and programming was just one more field. Would it surprise you to learn that at age twelve, Zuckerberg began connecting his own family – his first social grouping?

"Zucknet" interconnected the computers of his family and their businesses so they could more easily communicate, support, and bond with each other. His passion for relationship-building began in his childhood and has never stopped.

Should Facebook disappear tomorrow, Mark would continue to promote the quality of life and success of individuals en masse through bonding people. Technology was only a convenient tool of his savant domain but not that domain.

It is his passion for relationship-building that prompted a computer science geek at Harvard to also take psychology. Mark's *raison d'être* is to elevate the quality of life of people around the world by improving their connections and relationships. He is driven to unify, better, and bond humanity.

Shaping evolution

Each of these six superachievers had a biological predisposition to the personal savant domain for which they later became celebrated. That field of genius was often evident before they were five years old but certainly by the time they entered their teens.

Imagine decades of peak-performance and peak-growth savantflows within their savant domains starting this young. Imagine the success of your career if you never left your savant domain from birth to death. It is easy to see why competitors could never keep pace with these icons.

Notice that, for the four technology founders, the fields in which they became renowned really didn't exist to any extent until they created or developed them. Notice as well that each of their savant domains was beneficial to humanity. This is what you would expect if people are partnered with the evolutionary forces of the bioflow continuously mutating, adapting and advancing the human species for survival.

Nature will provide support based not only on the maximizing of your system but also the maximizing of humanity's system. The bioflow will guide you to maximizing both simultaneously – to the perfect intersection of two hierarchical systems maximizing. This is the formula for your greatest support from the bioflow to achieve your goals.

This is what you will learn from the six iconic savant-domain career models examined in this book. *They each excelled in a savant domain that was facilitating the ideal direction of human evolution.* This is the ideal strategy for yourself or any company you might run.

5

Born into the Bioflow

In this chapter and the next, I want to introduce nonsavant groups with the same external information access as is behind the superskills of savants. You might not have realized how many groups there are because they haven't been linked before with each other or with savants. This evidence will reinforce my proposal that we may all be able to access savant genius.

If I demonstrate the prevalence of this access capability, the question then becomes, "What are savants and these groups of nonsavants doing differently from the rest of us to trigger spontaneous information inflow?" Perhaps addressing this next question will help us with this one – "Why did evolution select for this spontaneous information sourcing capability?"

If I have argued successfully, I believe you'll have the answer to both questions by the final chapter. It is entitled *Our Savant-Domain Creational Purpose*. The success of the human species relies on the creativity which generates its adaptivity. Creativity is the re-combining of existing information systems to create a new information system which is a solution, creation, invention, or innovation.

The access to spontaneous information demonstrated by savants is the first step in the process. It is the fuel for our adaptive creativity. With a degree in bioanthropology, I tend to think with evolution's mindset. I tend to apply my knowledge of running large multinationals to evolution's strategic purposes.

Our survival individually and collectively relies on adaptivity. Since our information access increases with connection to the bioflow, we can assume that this connection is relevant to our quest. To connect with the bioflow we need to be operating at our maximum – savantflow.

Studies show that creativity increases even in regular flow states. It is reasonable to assume that creativity would be even stronger during the more meaningful and enticing work of applying or enhancing one's strongest talents in savantflow.

Without savantflows, the second part of the creative process is compromised – our ability to re-combine the information fuel is greatly reduced. Evolution seems to have selected for a plethora of mutations and adaptations within the human body to not only support this two-part creational process but to make it irresistible. We therefore have the beginnings of a working hypothesis to be investigated.

Bioflow-based information access in preschoolers

The Land study below suggests to me that we are born fully integrated into the bioflow, but our enculturation process removes that connection. At birth, we are merged with the surrounding bio-infrastructure and operate with our full internal-external potential. We must be taught to become separate human beings who end at our skin. The detachment of the majority of us from the bioflow seems to coincide with entry into the school system at age five.

Many preschool children have surprised their parents by communicating wisdom or information to which they know their children have never been exposed. Just as with savants, they are demonstrating access to external information which they did not absorb through their five senses. They are outperforming their assumed potential.

To measure the decline in our savant-like genius when we detach from the bioflow, consider the now-famous Land study. In the sixties, NASA conducted a highly specialized creativity test to improve their hiring practices for the space program. Inadvertently, this test showed that we are born creative and society "degeniuses" them.[16]

> *Everyone is born a genius, but the process of living*
> *de-geniuses them.*   R. Buckminster Fuller

Dr. George Land, a highly respected University of Minnesota professor and Pulitzer Prize nominated author, was commissioned to design the long-term study. He found the following decline in creativity:[17]

- **Creative genius in 5-year-olds: 98%**
- **Creative genius in 10-year-olds: 30%**
- **Creative genius in 15-year-olds: 12%**
- **Creative genius in 280,000 adults, average age 31:   2%**

A preliminary glimpse of our six superachievers – Bill Gates, Steve Jobs, Jeff Bezos, Mark Zuckerberg, Oprah Winfrey, and Jim Carrey – shows that they all operated in the savant domains of their future success from childhood. *The evidence suggests that they never disconnected from the bioflow*. That is why I selected them for study.

Therefore, these six icons had had decades of savantflows increasing their functionality and expanding their consciousnesses before they even entered the public eye. Our six superachievers are all intelligent, but would they have had the genius behind their success if they had not exploited the bioflow in their savant domain?

Savant episodes

Developmental psychologist Joseph Chilton Pearce is the grandfather of the conscious parenting movement. In his book "Evolution's End" (1992), Pearce recounts a story from his own life that demonstrates what he calls a "savant episode." It serves as another example of external information inflow, but this time from a nonsavant with normal intelligence.

In his early thirties, Pearce was obsessed with the nature of the God-human relationship – a key thrust of his savant domain. One morning his five-year-old son came into his room and launched into a 20-minute speech on the nature of God and man. "He spoke in perfect, publishable sentences," Pearce writes, "without pause or haste, and in a flat monotone. He used complex theological terminology and told me, it seemed, everything there was to know.

"As I listened, astonished, the hair rose on my neck; I felt goose bumps, and, finally, tears streamed down my face. I was in the midst of the uncanny, the inexplicable. My son's ride to kindergarten arrived, horn blowing, and he got up and left.

"I was unnerved and arrived late to my class. What I had heard was awesome, but too vast and far beyond any concept I had had to that point. The gap was so great I could remember almost no details and little of the broad panorama he had presented. My son had no recollection of the event."[18]

Pearce speculated on how his son's enlightening communication might have occurred. His son was a bright, normal child. At age five, his son had presented a field of knowledge which he could not have acquired – just as with savants.

"Terms such as telepathy are misleading," Pearce warns. "He wasn't picking up his materials from me. I hadn't acquired anything like what he described and would, in fact, be in my mid-fifties and involved in meditation before I did."

Pearce came to believe that his son had come into the influence of Pearce's field of concern and the larger ancient field of theological and psychological inquiry. "My son's theological discourse was not random but squarely in keeping with my own passionate pursuits," Pearce claims.[19]

Since the information was beyond Pearce's knowledge and comprehension at the time, psi or ESP could not have been a possible explanation. Therefore, Pearce concluded that his son must have undergone a "savant episode."

Bioflow-driven savant episodes

Savanting offers another explanation. It is not his son who was driving the savant episode but Pearce himself. Pearce was operating in his savant domain exploring the nature of the God-human relationship. He was likely in savantflow operating at his maximum at the time. He was therefore connected to the bioflow which brings spontaneous information related to the activity generating the savantflow.

The savant episode was an example of support by the bioflow. This support includes providing information for your progress or growth through a multitude of sources. Such information might present through clusters of information coincidences, models of solutions, and facilitating people and events, for example.

Through his son, Pearce had access to information relevant to the goals of his savantflow within his savant domain in a slightly different way than savants. However, the same principles apply.

As an aside I should point out that Pearce unfortunately didn't realize that the information his son conveyed was state-bound to Pearce's very deep savantflow. He therefore did not immediately document the information so he could review it in his normal consciousness in order to retain it.

As you become the creative worldchanger you were meant to be, you'll want to make it a habit to capture all your spontaneous knowledge during or immediately after your savantflows.

The first time I recognized that I was experiencing the type of savant episode Pearce has described was in 1992 when I had been operating in my savant domain for a little over a year. I had already recognized that my savantflows were getting deeper and more profound over that time. In this particular savantflow, I was stumped as to how biology was working in a certain situation.

A co-worker with negligible knowledge of biology opened my office door, stuck his head in, gave me the answer and then promptly closed the door again. He used the same monotone that Pearce noted for his son. To this day Jack has no idea why he did it, where he got the information, what he said, or even what the information meant when I repeated it back to him at a later date.

There is an additional part to savanting's explanation of Pearce's savant episode. In this chapter you are beginning to see evidence that we are all born into the bioflow and must be taught to separate from it by our cultural institutions and our parents. Therefore, preschool children tend to still be connected to the bioflow. As a result, they do indeed come out with information they have not absorbed through their five senses.

Pearce's five-year-old son was still connected to and compliant with the bioflow. He thus became an instrument of the bioflow for providing the information that Pearce needed for the work of his savantflow. Preschool children thus become an excellent conduit for externally sourced savant genius for advancing one's work in one's savant domain.

I suspect that Jack became an instrument of the bioflow like Pearce's son because he too was working in his savant domain and thus complying with the orchestration of the bioflow. Therefore, we can assume that the instruments for savant episodes are people connected to the bioflow. However, there is one more unexpected explanation for Pearce's savant episode.

Savant Episodes vs information coincidences

First, I want to take a moment to differentiate savant episodes from information coincidences. Information coincidences will abound as soon as you begin savanting. When you are complying with the directional information of the bioflow you will be colliding with the right information at the right time for meeting savant-domain goals.

This means you will experience a multitude of seemingly serendipitous information events such as opening a book at the right page; flipping on the right TV channel at the right time; meeting a person with the exact answer you need; or clicking on an internet news item with the exact model for the solution to your goal.

Savanting is an entirely different paradigm of operation. Information coincidences are so prevalent in a serial-savantflow life that you'll find yourself building into your project planning timeframes your accelerated progress as a result of expecting them. Their absence from other sectors of your life makes pursuing a life in your savant domain all the more enticing.

However, the savant episode that Pearce describes or my experience with Jack is a whole other level of mystical magic. This is a real person who gives you the answer you need without knowing they are doing it or having ever sourced that information in their past.

Information is nonlocal

What is the explanation for savant episodes and our increased access to information through savanting? Let me quote myself from a section entitled "All Information is Distributed" in "Peak Evolution: Beyond Peak Performance and Peak Experience" (2001, 2010):

"As we learned in investigating the knowledge technology, quantum physics proposes that all information is distributed or nonlocal. There is no local information or localized memory.

"It is a law of information theory that information transcends time and space, placing it beyond the confining limits of matter and energy. I thus hypothesized a holographic interconnection of all information. A universal information hologram into which we, as information systems, are integrated."[20]

Albert Einstein reinforced this concept, "Time and space are modes by which we think, not conditions in which we live." This is an important distinction.

Michael Talbot was the author of a book which was catalytic in launching my development of savanting. In "The Holographic Universe," Talbot concurred with Einstein, "Challenging evidence is being offered from a number of different directions that information, not mass or energy, is the ultimate fabric of the cosmos."[21]

Many have heard from physicists that information is nonlocal but have not incorporated the possibilities of this fact into their belief system to augment their access to relevant information. In fact, many assume they only have access to local information absorbed through their five senses. This belief therefore limits the reality that they can experience. Savanting provides the means to get practical about the application of nonlocalized information.

Alternative explanation of savant episodes

Therefore, I want to offer an uncommon explanation for Pearce's savant episode which requires neither the spiritual nor religious disciplines normally associated with this subject matter.

There is a growing body of evidence developed by psychologists and consciousness researchers about the altered states of consciousness which are associated with even normal flow states. These are enhanced, accelerated, and amplified in savantflows. Over time savantflows become deeper, more productive, more creative, more profound, more mystical, and more expansive.

Consciousness continues to expand until suddenly you will experience cosmic-consciousness events in which you are one with everything. As you progress, you'll eventually find that, in your deepest savantflows, you can enter cosmic consciousness at will when it is beneficial to the activity which has incited your savantflow. These states are much easier to achieve through savantflow than any form of meditation.

If one shifts into unity consciousness or cosmic consciousness in one's savantflow only a single consciousness will exist. Therefore, Joseph Chilton Pearce and his son would have been a single consciousness having a single epiphany during a savant episode that was Pearce's not his son's.

Consequently, we may assume that the powers and potential of humanity may be greater than I have alluded to this point. They are greater than what is indicated by the existence of savants. The normal state of consciousness of future humans may be far different than what is prevalent today. Instead of visiting cosmic consciousness from today's normal consciousness, we may instead be visiting normal consciousness from living life predominantly from expanded consciousness.

Needless to say, we are going to want to educate, enculturate, and nurture our children very differently in the future to retain the bioflow connection demonstrated by our six superachievers. Anyone wanting their children to achieve their true internal-external potential will want to identify and cultivate their child's savant formula.

There are more examples of external information access by other categories of nonsavants in the next chapter. They will reinforce the hypothesis that the fuel behind savant genius is externally sourced and therefore accessible to all of us regardless of our intelligence, talents, or aptitudes.

In our inner being, we are one with all.   Swami Dhyan Giten

Everything exists as information in a field of infinite possibilities, and it is our Consciousness that renders the information and causes it to appear as the material world.   Joseph P. Kauffman

The fundamental delusion of humanity is to suppose that I am here and you are out there.   Yasutani Roshi, Zen master (1885-1973)

---

[16]   *Coert Engels, We are born creative geniuses and the education system dumbs us down, according to NASA scientists, 2017,*
https://ideapod.com/born-creative-geniuses-education-system-dumbs-us-according-nasa-scientists/
and David Williams, NASA scientists: People are born "creative geniuses" but get dumbed down by the U.S. education system, February 5, 2018
https://space.news/2018-02-05-nasa-scientists-people-are-born-creative-geniuses-but-get-dumbed-down-by-education-system.html

[17]   Nick Skillicorn, *Evidence that children become less creative over time (and how to fix it),* August 5th, 2016
[18]   Joseph Chilton Pearce, *Evolution's End,* 1992 In: San Francisco, CA: HarperSanFrancisco; p. 8-9
[19]   Joseph Chilton Pearce, *Evolution's End,* 1992 p. 9-10
[20]   Lauren Holmes (2001/2010) *Peak Evolution: Beyond Peak Performance and Peak Experience:* Chapter 11: *The Power of Emotion*
[21]   Michael Talbot, *The Holographic Universe,* 1991, HarperCollins Publishers

6

Savant-Like Information Access by NonSavants

I conjectured previously that savants were able to access "books" or complete systems of information associated with their savant domain. In fact, it seemed to me that the various categories of savants were accessing the same "book." We appear to have lots of categories of nonsavants also accessing "books" of information from a broad range of savant domains. This augurs well for all of us to source the information necessary to fuel our own savant genius.

NonSavant access to *"books"* of information

Savant capabilities suggest an increased potential for all of us. If one group of human beings is capable of superior access to the information behind savant superskills then it is reasonable to assume we all are. Therefore, we would expect to see lots of additional categories of people besides savants who are able to access the encyclopedic and procedural information which savants do.

As you will see in the groups of people below, this indeed appears to be the case. But here is what is intriguing. As with the savant domains of Gates, Jobs, Zuckerberg, Bezos, Winfrey, and Carrey, many of these additional groups likely also spend a lot of time in savantflows within their savant domains.

This would put them into their biological maximum and thus reconnect them with the bioflow. External biological mechanisms, capabilities, and information databases would therefore extend their own capabilities.

What we are seeing across savants and many categories of nonsavants is an identical formula for savant-level, information-fueled skills. The altered consciousness of savantflow seems to quell the left-brain gatekeeping in nonsavants to that of savants with left-brain damage. Savantflow brains and savant brains seem to have similar capabilities.

Notice that the "book" access by the following groups falls into three categories: *personbooks*, *factbooks*, and *procedurebooks*. A "personbook" is the complete system of information about a person which includes their personality, their knowledge, and their physicality. A "factbook" holds a system of encyclopedic information. A "procedurebook" is the system of information and skills for performing an activity.

Personbooks

Multiple personality disorder

Those with multiple personality disorder (MPD) – or, as it is now called, dissociative identity disorder (DID) – often have personalities knowledgeable in different languages or complex fields of study *to which the Multiple, like the savant, has never been exposed.*

This is a bizarre syndrome in which two or more distinct personalities inhabit a single body. It is akin to changing the software running one's body. Most Multiples average between eight to thirteen personalities, although so-called superMultiples may have more than a hundred subpersonalities.

There is compelling clinical data showing that alternate personalities can be concurrently conscious and see themselves as distinct identities. It's as if they downloaded one or more new "personbooks" as and when circumstances arose requiring the services of different personalities or physicality.

How adaptive is that! Imagine the direction of human evolution if everyone is able to download the "personbook" they need to negotiate the various situations in their lives! An athlete personality for your workouts. A dealmaker personality to get you that next raise. A brilliant expert to write your exams. A person fluent in languages for your international travel, and so on.

Maybe MPD is how future-human expanded consciousness will work. This is a new spin on the true potential of human beings. The future talent wars would not be about recruiting the person born with the best talents, but the person who can access the breadth of knowledge and skills of multiple persons.

Even the bodies of Multiples source new information from the "personbook" download as well. Each personality routinely has its own physical abilities, IQ, voice characteristics, brainwave patterns, biochemistry, blood-flow patterns, heart rate, scars, and left- and right-handedness.

Visual acuity can differ requiring some Multiples to carry two or three different pairs of eyeglasses to accommodate their alternating personalities. One personality can be colorblind and another not. Even eye color can change. With a personality shift, a Multiple who is drunk may suddenly sober.

Allergies associated with one personality may disappear completely with another. There are cases of women having two or three menstrual periods per month due to each subpersonality having its own cycle.

If an adult personality is given a drug and then a child's personality takes over, the adult dosage will cause an overdose. It is difficult to anesthetize some Multiples. There are accounts of Multiples waking up on the operating table after one of their "unanesthetizable" subpersonalities has taken over.

The flexibility of the human body to match the beliefs of the active personality is astounding. Wouldn't it be great if we could download an MPD alternate who is lean, fit, and healthy? We may never have to work out or diet again.

Did the Multiple simply access a "personbook" that contained all of the knowledge and specifications of each of the living or dead, fictional or nonfictional "people" that he or she becomes? Is the Multiple simply an avatar for the "personbook" accessed? There is, as yet, no scientific explanation for the source and completeness of each personality that emerges in Multiples.

For us, however, we are seeing the same access to external information systems demonstrated by savants. These "books," though, are simply not restricted to the five or so major domains available to savants.

Reincarnation in children

Sourcing an external "personbook" would also explain the phenomenon whereby children have been known to have the complete knowledge of a deceased person's life. These instances have often been cited as confirmation of reincarnation.

There is an alternate explanation. Could young children – who have not yet acquired the gatekeeping, rule-driven, left brains of adults – have simply accessed a person's "book" from the external library? "Yes!" Let me add another convincing twist.

Just as with Multiples, the same biological changes occur as part of the download of the dead person's "personbook." Their physicality changes to match those of the person whose book they have accessed – albeit with less compliance than with Multiples.

Dr. Ian Stevenson was the former Chairman of the Department of Psychiatry at the University of Virginia Medical School. In the early sixties, he gave up his prestigious position to investigate cases of children's spontaneous past life memories and other paranormal phenomena. For more than 40 years, Dr. Stevenson traveled around the world rigorously documenting between 2,500 and 3,000 cases of young children who had spontaneous recall of the verifiable lives of others.

Dr. Stevenson found a physical correspondence between lifetimes. In 1997, he published a weighty, two-volume, 2,200-page tome called "Reincarnation and Biology." He documents 225 cases of birthmarks and birth defects on children which corresponded to fatal wounds, injuries, or illnesses of the person the children remembered being in their supposed former life. These children gave enough specific detail about their former lives (proper names, locations, descriptions of their deaths) that their "former identities" could be verified.

Did you know that each new incarnation of the Dalai Lama is determined by testing the past life memories of several young candidates? They look for the reincarnation of the previous Dalai Lama. If the child can correctly identify people and possessions known to the former Dalai Lama, they know they have identified their next Dalai Lama.

Enlightenment

Now here is a novel thought. Isn't enlightenment the moment you access the "book" about yourself? According to Lao Tzu, "He who knows others is wise; he who knows himself is enlightened."

A synonymous term in Zen, "kensho," means "seeing into one's true nature."

In the West, enlightenment has become synonymous with self-realization and the true self. Are you ready to be enlightened? Can you download your own "personbook?" Spontaneous enlightenment and self-knowledge of one's purpose and lifework are other examples of "book" downloads. They leave people as redirected to self-actualization as those who've had a near death experience.

Or did you download a "personbook" when you were born and you now simply need to become conscious of it to be enlightened? Or did we each choose the "personbook" or "person system" through which we were going to channel cosmic consciousness.

In any event, extreme self-knowledge is a byproduct of the proposed bioflow partnering process whether it is downloaded as a "personbook" or not. You'll learn many things about yourself and your true identity when you figure out how nature's machinery is trying to maximize and adapt your system. In addition, there is nothing like the expanded consciousness that comes with the bioflow partnering to shed light on the real "you."

Actor Jim Carrey channeled the Andy Kaufman "Book?"

Carrey won a Golden Globe award for the biopic "Man on the Moon" (1999). Many in the know say that Jim was so good at the role that he must have channeled comedian Andy Kaufman. His manner, bearing, speech, and idiosyncrasies were accurate even though Jim had never met Andy.

In addition, it is as if Carrey replaced his own body software by downloading the entire "personbook" of Andy Kaufman's physicality and personality. So much so, that Jim remained in character on and off set for the duration of making the movie. To get his attention, one needed to call "Andy." He seemed to no longer recognize "Jim" as his name. Carrey could only access one "personbook" at a time.

Oprah accessed preacher and sermon "books?"

Could Oprah's recitation of powerful sermons at three and a half years old be due to accessing the "personbook" of the speaker and/or sermon "factbook" she was reciting? Or, did she actually memorize these sermons? Oprah says she provided all the emotion and animation of the original preacher even though she admits she didn't always know what was said.

Because as a child Oprah loved preaching so much and because she was using her strongest talents in her savant domain, she would have been routinely maximized in savantflow. This would have facilitated information access. What do you think? Did pre-school Oprah speak from her own memory or an external memory?

Psychic and medium personbooks

Despite a field strewn with frauds, most of us have encountered, live or through media, at least one psychic who was the real thing. The real ones are operating in their savant domain. In savantflow state, they will be able to download the "personbook" of their client as well as relevant "personbooks" and "factbooks" associated with their client's life.

The same is true of those who claim to "speak" to the dead or those who "channel" them. By adjusting their state of being to the altered consciousness of savantflow they increase their ability to access relevant "personbooks" to know information about the lives of dead people.

You have probably seen the tests that measure if one is psychic. The participant is asked to guess what color or shape is hiding under a card. If one guesses correctly enough times, the results indicate that this individual has a high probability of being psychic.

Many psychics score poorly on these tests. They do no better than anyone else. Yet, the very same psychics, when reading for their clients, may have an uncanny ability to describe past and future situations and events with a fair degree of accuracy.

The tests of psychic abilities are not valid if the individual cannot enter savantflow to access external information. The psychic needs to be able to go into savantflow while using their strongest talents in their savant domain.

This is what will trigger access to "personbooks" to provide the necessary information to do what they love to do. Current psychic tests prohibit flow state and they don't invoke the passion that working with a live client will.

Client personbooks

Many professionals whose savant domain includes the in-depth analysis of individuals may routinely slip into savantflow and access the client's "personbook." I find I often download "personbooks" in my work to design and implement biologically maximized careers. In fact, when working in savantflow with a client, the only "personbook" open is that of the client. I cease to exist as a separate entity in identityless, egoless flow states.

Once I'm deep enough into savantflow, I'm able to see the entirety of the client's "personbook" as a continuum from childhood to the present. I "know" things they haven't told me or I can deduce them. I experience their emotional events as if they had been my own. I know what the bioflow has and has not supported in their past.

I'm not psychic. However, I can appear to be. The ideal projection of the client's savant domain into the future becomes obvious to me and too logical for a client to refute. Accordingly, I can generate the ideal contexts and strategies which will garner future bioflow support and continuously raise the bar on the client's self-actualization and self-transcendence.

Factbooks and Procedurebooks

Simultaneous discovery/invention/creation in multiple locations
Downloading the same "factbook" or "procedurebook" for a savant domain is a possible explanation for the phenomenon of simultaneous scientific discoveries or inventions in multiple locations throughout the world. The hypothesis here would be that multiple individuals working in their savant domain in savantflow simultaneously access the same relevant state-of-the-art "factbook" from the "library" or database defining humanity.

When they access the information piece they are missing, they can re-combine it with their existing information from their field to generate new information, a new solution, a new invention, or a new discovery. If the related pieces can only be re-combined in the same way or they are part of an obvious trend for the field, it is likely that more than one person knowledgeable in the field with come up with the same invention, innovation, or creation.

Near-death and out-of-body experience
Experts in near death experiences such as Elizabeth Kubler-Ross, Raymond Moody, Ken Ring, and P.M.H. Atwater have accumulated so much research on those who've had near death experiences (NDEs) that it has almost become a science of facts. Anecdotal reports from those who've had near-death experiences (NDEs) describe their ability to access complete fields of

information or "books" as soon as they focus on them. The same is true of those who've cultivated astral projection or out-of-body experiences (OBEs).

Many NDEs and OBEs have described these experiences as all-knowingness or omniscience. I think it would be more accurate to continue to use the metaphor of checking a "book" out of the library for each subject on which they focus their attention. It is likely that the altered states of consciousness of these two states are similar to savantflow and thus promote information inflow.

Remote viewing

Remote viewing is the practice of seeking impressions about a distant or unseen target using subjective means, specifically, extrasensory perception (ESP) or "sensing with mind." Accordingly, it was heavily tested by the military with seeming success. However, others claim there is no credible scientific evidence that remote viewing works and regard it as pseudoscience.

Remote-viewing believers and practitioners now have an alternate explanation and an alternate methodology for pursuing its goals – accessing the relevant "factbook" of the distant or unseen target while in savantflow or similar altered state of consciousness which turns off the left-brain gatekeeper.

Perhaps the disagreement on its success results from the wrong test as in the case of psychics. The practitioners that failed the tests were not able to get into the flow state around the work they are passionate about doing. They were therefore not able to access the necessary "factbooks."

Prodigies are higher IQ savants

Prodigies display adult competency as children. They are easily recognized. Mozart composed his first piece of music at age five. Picasso finished his first painting at nine. Math genius

William James Sidis entered Harvard at age eleven. Oprah orated sermons at age three and a half. Prodigies have savant-level skills that are equally superhuman. And, "Yes", they too have a savant domain like all savants and nonsavants.

In keeping with our hypothesis behind savant-level skills, prodigies also spend a tremendous amount of time in savantflow within their savant domain. This could provide access to the massive information they need for their savant-like skills. It also could explain why they too seem to "know" things in their savant domain which they have not learned.

There is different jargon associated with the study of prodigies, but I believe we are still dealing with the same mechanisms I have been describing for savants and for the six superachievers examined in this book. Prodigy expert Martha J. Morelock suggests that all prodigies have a demonstrated "rage to learn."

I think this rage might be explained by the addictive nature of high-growth savantflows. Each of the six savant-domain careers was driven by the same addiction. It is well documented that the four tech founders often worked through the night without food, drink, or sleep sustained totally by the addictive nature of savantflows. Flow is not only a peak performance state but a peak learning state. One must be stretched beyond one's previous capabilities in order to enter flow.

Prodigies have been identified as having extraordinary working memories – defined as not just the ability to remember something but the ability to hold and manipulate various pieces of information at a time. I believe this is common in savantflow for nonsavants as well.

Studies do not yet identify the source of the information internally for manipulation in their working memories. Therefore, I believe we are free to make the case for externally sourced knowledge here as well.

Your own Aha! moments

I've already suggested that the internal-external partnership will increase one's experience of information leaps. Leaps are another example of downloading large systems or "books" of information spontaneously. Many of us have had experiences of suddenly knowing whole systems of information. Think of your own moments of insight or epiphany. Consider your Eureka! or Aha! events.

Consider your times of suddenly knowing how something works or the procedural information for how to achieve a goal or how all the pieces fit together. You too have undoubtedly sourced an in-depth, already integrated "personbook," "procedurebook," or "factbook" from humanity's hologram through various leaps.

Your flashes of genius may enable you to perceive beyond your current capabilities – to outperform your potential. You'll know this all-to-well if you forget to capture state-bound information before you leave your savantflow. All that you'll remember is the emotional feel of brilliance with no ability to reconstruct the breakthrough.

Future human consciousness?

Since the exponential growth of the internet, human consciousness has been expanding more rapidly than at any other point in the history of civilization. More people have been thinking globally on a routine basis than ever before.

Rather than being damaged or defective as so many think, those with MPD may in fact be a symptom of expanding human consciousness en route to unity consciousness. They are demonstrating the capabilities of evolving humans.

Pearce's savant episode as a product of unity consciousness is another version of future functionality. Children who can simultaneously open their own personbook and that of someone who has died are another example.

If you look through the perspective of unity or cosmic consciousness, one cannot help but notice that the universe itself has multiple personality disorder. A single consciousness flicks through the perspective of the 7.7 billion people who live on Earth. One consciousness has access to 7.7 billion "personbooks." We each are an alternate personality. World peace would be much more achievable with this model.

One has to ask then if multiple personality disorder has evolved in the image of a multi-person model of the universal consciousness. Imagine if this multi-person perspective became the new consciousness of a global leader or manager. Imagine if future leaders could operate with this breadth of consciousness through the perspective of their various followers at will. Imagine if they could remote view their competition.

As creative beings, this may be a highly productive evolutionary advance to expand the talents we might apply to our creational projects. Perhaps just such an expansion to the model of psychic mediums, allows us to extend our personal talent pool beyond those living on earth currently.

When you look at all the examples of "personbook" downloads, it is difficult not to see a trend. In addition, they are simply externally sourced information systems. It may be easier to identify "personbooks" access. However, it would be illogical to not assume that other information systems are not similarly downloadable.

The information access behind the savant genius we want to experience and exploit is now appearing more logical than the alternative – *not* being able to source information systems externally.

III

SIGNS OF SAVANTING

DID THESE ICONS SUCCEED WITH SAVANTING?

JIM CARREY	comedian, entertainer, actor, impressionist, screenwriter, film producer
OPRAH	media mogul, talk show host, actress, producer, philanthropist
STEVE JOBS	co-founder of Apple, information technology entrepreneur, inventor, a pioneer of the microcomputer revolution, Pixar computer-animation pioneer
BILL GATES	co-founder of Microsoft, information technology entrepreneur, mega-philanthropist pioneer, computer programmer, a pioneer of the microcomputer revolution
JEFF BEZOS	founder of Amazon.com, business leader, entrepreneur, e-commerce pioneer, aerospace pioneer
MARK ZUCKERBERG	co-founder of Facebook, internet entrepreneur, social networking pioneer, philanthropist

Chapters

7

Jim Carrey: Paid Play

Jim Carrey on the internal-external partnership:

I used to believe that who I was ended at the edge of my skin. That I had been given this little vehicle called a body from which to experience creation. And though I couldn't have asked for a sportier model, it was after all a loaner and would have to be returned. And then I learned that everything outside of the vehicle was part of me too. And now I drive a convertible.

Excerpted from Jim Carrey's commencement address at the 2014 Maharishi University of Management Graduation

JIM CARREY'S $10 MILLION CHECK

Jim Carrey has become a renowned entertainer, comedian, and actor. So many achievement junkies have been inspired by the story of a depressed, broke, and pre-success Jim writing a $10 million check to himself in 1985 as part of his creative visualization process. He marked the check's memo, "For services rendered."

Jim was attempting to motivate himself as he stood on Mulholland Drive overlooking the splendor of the Hollywood Hills. The 23-year-old postdated the check 10 years out for Thanksgiving 1995 hoping that he'd be in a position to cash it by then.

Carrey's optimism and tenacity did indeed pay off by 1995 as you can see by his salary per film in this table from IMDB.com.

1990	In Living Color	$25,000/episode
1994	Ace Ventura: Pet Detective	$350,000
1994	The Mask	$540,000
1994	Dumb & Dumber	$7,000,000
1995	Batman Forever	$7,000,000
1995	Ace Ventura: When Nature Calls	$15,000,000
1996	The Cable Guy	$20,000,000
1997	Liar Liar	$20,000,000

Following "In Living Color," Jim's transformation from TV goofball to marquee headliner happened within a single year. His spectacular breakthrough year was 1994, the year before his check was dated. He had the distinction of becoming the first actor to have three films go straight to number one in one year: "Ace Ventura: Pet Detective," "The Mask," and "Dumb & Dumber."

His $20 million salary for "The Cable Guy" in 1996 was the largest up-front sum that had ever been offered to any comedic actor. Carrey has had eight Golden Globes nominations and two wins. He is among the few who've won the Best Actor awards in both Drama and Comedy – in 1998 for "The Truman Show" and in 1999 for "Man on the Moon."

The true goal of Jim's $10 million check

Many misinterpret the Jim-Carrey-check event. The money was not the true goal of the $10 million check. The check was a metaphor. A symbol of a desired emotional state and circumstance. What Jim truly craved atop the Hollywood Hills was the opportunity to do the work he loves and for which he is not only biologically predisposed but frankly addicted. He wanted to do intrinsically or biologically rewarding work – work that was its own reward.

He wanted to uplift audiences, to improve their lives, to help them forget their troubles for a while. He had sought to do this for his parents, his family, his friends, and strangers since his preschool years. In Jim's own words, "What I have in common with the character in "Truman" is this incredible need to please people. I feel like I want to take care of everyone and I also feel this terrible guilt if I am unable to. And I have felt this way ever since all this success started."

Carrey also craved industry experts valuing his work to the tune of $10 million. He wanted to impress those with the credentials to know he had done good work. He wanted to impress himself by continuously surpassing his previous performances. The goal of the $10 million check was to get the work that would enable Jim to operate at his maximum in his savant domain of bringing joy to audiences.

Does anyone doubt that Jim Carrey was biologically wired to be an entertainer? Is there any question that he has found a way to use his strongest most rewarding talents for their most meaningful and valued application?

Jim's $10-million-check goal was only achieved because the work Jim was trying to do was not simply the work he loved but happened to be the same work that would maximize him. Accordingly, the additional resources of the bioflow would thus kick in to facilitate his progress.

You will see shortly that the same is true of Oprah, Bill Gates, Steve Jobs, Jeff Bezos, and Mark Zuckerberg. They share(d) the same formula for success. *Their success came from applying their strongest, most meaningful, most emotionally rewarding talents to the most meaningful and intrinsically rewarding tasks for the audience or context most valuing of their work.* In other words, *they pursued biologically maximized careers and lives in their savant domains.*

The same success formula explains how an unlikely movie star, Sylvester Stallone, orchestrated his breakthrough into acting by writing "Rocky" (1976) and insisting that he play the title role. Stallone was offered a fortune to sell the "Rocky" screenplay. He refused despite living in poverty at the time. The money was never the goal. As with Jim Carrey, the craving was for a particular kind of work through which the greatest creative expression of his essence could emerge.

Control of natural forces vs compliance with them?

With Jim's $10M check incident and Oprah's Color Purple story coming up, both felt these were examples of success through the law of attraction. For me, these were examples of savanting – choosing the types of goals which maximize their biological predisposition and attract the support of the bioflow throughout their lives.

These were goals consistent with moving each of them towards maximization and self-actualization. They were goals which advanced their savant domain. These were not new goals but an advancement of the life themes defining their savant domain.

Wikipedia defines the law of attraction as the belief that positive or negative thoughts bring positive or negative experiences into a person's life. People and their thoughts are both believed to be made from pure energy. Since they believe "like energy attracts like energy," positive thoughts should attract improved health, wealth, personal relationships, and other goals.

According to their philosophy, to effectively change one's negative thinking patterns, one must use creative visualization to "feel" that the desired changes have already occurred. This combination of positive thought and positive emotion is believed to allow one to attract positive experiences and opportunities.

To improve your own skills for goal achievement, you'll want to decide whether Jim and Oprah bent the forces of the universe to their will with the law of attraction. Did they redirect the immutable forces of the universe to achieve their goals? Or was their success simply from pursuing the greatest expression of their biological predisposition. Was their success instead from sustaining a birth-to-death partnership with the bioflow maximizing machinery?

Were these two dramatic events – Jim's $10M check incident and Oprah's Color Purple story – singular or part of the life themes of their savant domain continuum?

In this chapter and the next, let's examine Jim's life in greater depth for savanting patterns to help you determine the best answer for yourself.

CHILDHOOD PLAY TO ADULT PAID PLAY

There is a sweet spot where the application of talent and task match so perfectly that work becomes play. It exists where your strongest constellation of talents meets a task, a purpose, a meaning, and an audience perfectly suited to its maximum use. I'm certain you've all experienced its addictive elation.

This sweet spot is your savant domain. The ultimate career strategy then is "paid play" in your savant domain. No one symbolizes the idea of "paid play" better than Jim Carrey. But you'll find that each of these superachievers lived in this sweet spot and succeeded because of it.

As a child, Jim Carrey would perform constantly for anyone who would watch. In junior high, an insightful teacher granted him a few precious moments at the end of each school day in which to do stand-up routines for his classmates. This was an incentive offered in exchange for him behaving himself for the rest of the day. There was nothing Jim craved more.

Jim wore his tap shoes to bed just in case his troubled parents needed cheering up in the middle of the night. He applied to "The

Carol Burnett Show" in 1967 when he was just ten. He began performing in comedy clubs when he was sixteen.

There is no question that Carrey's $10 million check was a symbol of work well done in his savant domain. It represented paid play from doing the work that he was innately predisposed to do. He was born to entertain and addicted to it. This same biology-based addiction drove the careers of each of our superachievers. Their careers were propelled by project after project of intrinsically rewarding or biologically rewarding work.

> *Find your passion, and it's no longer work.* L.A Reid, *LaFace Records co-founder & CEO of Epic Records*

> *No man can be successful, unless he first loves his work.* David Sarnoff, CEO of RCA

> *The most beautiful fate, the most wonderful good fortune that can happen to any human being, is to be paid for doing that which he passionately loves to do.* Abraham Maslow

Jim Carrey Quotes

- *I learned many great lessons from my father, not the least of which is that you can fail at what you don't want, so you might as well take a chance on doing what you love.*
- *So many of us choose our path out of fear disguised as practicality. What we really want seems impossibly out of reach so we never dare to ask the universe for it. I'm the proof that you can ask the universe for it.*
- *I think everybody should get rich and famous and do everything they ever dreamed of so they can see that it's not the answer.*
- *My report card always said, "Jim finishes first and then disrupts the other students."*
- *Originality is really important . . . . Before I do anything, I think, well what hasn't been seen. Sometimes, that turns out to be*

something ghastly and not fit for society. And sometimes that inspiration becomes something that's really worthwhile.

- *I've arrived at the place if I'm not taking a career risk, I'm not happy. If I'm scared, then I know I'm being challenged.*
- *I absolutely want to have a career where you make 'em laugh and make 'em cry. It's all theater.*

8

Jim Carrey:
Support from the Bioflow

NATURE'S SELF-ORDERING PROCESS

One cannot study the human body without being in awe of how miraculously ordered it is – systems within systems and every system contributing to the maximization and continuous re-maximization of the whole for health and survival.

Similarly, one cannot investigate a biological ecosystem without admiring the same ordering of interrelated systems to ensure the balance and survival of the ecosystem. It would be illogical then to assume that these same ordering forces are not acting on us from the outside and pressuring us advantageously into the larger order of humanity, the planet, and the universe.

Capitalizing on these forces is where the power for savanting derives. They are knowable and predictable. Superachievers use them instinctively as we all did before cultural interference taught us to operate as separate entities.

Exploiting nature's self-ordering process within and around us offers another explanation for the success of Jim Carrey's check visualization and indeed how to speed goal achievement. First, let's look at what is behind the self-organizing. What is nature trying to accomplish?

Re-combining information for creativity and creation

The essence of nature's creativity for adapting, advancing, and continuously re-maximizing living systems for survival is the creativity formula already described – the re-combining of existing information systems to create a new system which solves an adaptation challenge or offers the next iteration of advance.

As a result, evolution and adaption progress by nonlinear leaps. The post-leap state is not predictable from the pre-leap state. This is why the leaps in your life – the breakthroughs, epiphanies, and coincidences – increase when you merge with the bioflow. We'll be exploiting leaps to speed you to your goals. One leap may bypass hundreds of steps.

To fuel the bioflow's adaptation assembly line, nature routinely self-organizes to group living systems together that will benefit from sharing each other's information and resources. If you want to increase the leaps in your life relevant to a goal, change the information structure of your system to be grouped with more advantageous systems.

The results of Jim's repositioning in the database

Our beliefs, emotions, genes, the biochemistry of epigenetics, and drives are the basics of the information storage units defining our system. When Jim Carrey wrote the $10 million check to strengthen his visualization, he changed his emotions and beliefs about what was possible for him. He changed the set of beliefs that defined his identity. This changed the information structure of his system.

As a result, nature's self-ordering librarian grouped Jim with new systems more relevant to his revised information structure and its new goals. Coincidences facilitating his goal began to emerge from his now being grouped with more advantageous systems.

For example, on the day Jim Carrey received the offer to do "Dumb & Dumber" for $350,000, "Ace Ventura: Pet Detective"

(1994), Carrey's first movie, coincidentally opened at the number one box office spot and stayed there for some time. The pursuant negotiations resulted in Jim receiving a final offer for $7 million for "Dumb & Dumber" which was almost half of the picture's $16 million budget.

It was also the most ever offered to a comedic actor according to the movie's director, Peter Farrelly. To put this leap and coincidence in perspective, the film's other headliner, Jeff Daniels, received a salary of only $50,000.

GUIDANCE BY THE BIOFLOW

This example demonstrates how the increased leaps and coincidences may also serve as a biological guidance system for one's savant-domain career by making the favorable directions for one's advance more obvious.

Clusters of leaps mean "Go." Blocks and frustrations mean "Stop," "Don't go," "Choose another direction" or "Delay your advance in this direction." If there are no telltale leaps guiding your life, you must have separated from the bioflow. You need to increase your savantflows to reconnect. Each opportunity for Jim to do the acting work he loves automatically puts him into serial savantflows which merge him with the bioflow.

The clustering of coincidences and facilitating events was an indicator from the bioflow that Jim should take the role in "Dumb & Dumber." It must be on his maximizing path. A significant pay raise was an indicator that the film was definitely a part of his savant-domain career. This is how the bioflow becomes a guidance system to help with one's decision-making and choice of directions.

Since you can see the indicators of what became success in this Jim Carrey example, you can start to watch for the same indicators in your reality to help with your own decision-making and pathfinding. For coincidences to even exist, one may assume one is moving with nature's assembly line producing them. They are produced when existing information systems are re-combined to create a new system.

The Farrelly brothers were the directors, producers and screenwriters for the Jim Carrey movies "Dumb & Dumber" (1994), "Dumb & Dumber To" (2014), and "Me, Myself & Irene" (2000). They were catalysts for the 1994 leap of Jim's salary from $540,000 for "The Mask" to $7 million for "Dumb & Dumber." We must therefore assume that nature's librarian grouped the revised Jim with the Farrelly brothers to further his savant-domain career.

The Farrelly brothers are living systems which could catalyze Carrey's visualized goal using the $10-million check. As synergistic information systems, the brothers' goals are also met by Carrey. It would therefore be completely logical for nature the librarian to group all three together to advance their respective savant domains to maximization.

Guided action after goal setting

In Jim's words from his study of the law of attraction, "As far as I can tell, it's just about letting the Universe know what you want, and working toward it, while letting go of how it comes to pass." However, he adds, "You can't just visualize and go eat a sandwich. You have to take action towards your goal."

Jim is deviating here from law-of-attraction principles with his advice. LOA followers declare that acting after visualization suggests you have no faith in the positive thinking and its ability for "like" to attract "like." Carrey's advice is trying to compensate for what he perceives as a flaw in their process.

LOA is not truly his way. Rather savanting is more consistent with Jim's formula for success. Savanting agrees with Jim's bias for action following goalsetting and the restructuring of one's information system. Savanting is 100% about taking action proactively in compliance with the bioflow. Savantflows cannot be invoked without doing an intrinsically rewarding task associated with improving your strongest talents or advancing your savant domain.

Savanting also helps with *what actions to take* after your visualization of your new goal. The bioflow is a guidance system leading you into the ideal direction for your system with respect to your new goal, your savant domain, and the evolution of humanity. But most importantly, complying with this guidance system directs you to the pieces of information that you can re-combine for breakthrough answers or creations.

For you to be able to harness the power of the bioflow machinery, one's goals must be formulated in such a way as to meet nature's goals for maximizing your system within nature's goals for maximizing humanity. Jim's $10M check was consistent with the goals of the internal-external maximizing machinery.

Imagine tying your career or your company to the machinery that is adapting and advancing the human race. You cannot help but always be leading-edge. This is a completely unprecedented guidance system for one's career, lifework, or company. Competitive advantage just got a little more interesting.

It is now undoubtedly more evident how Bill Gates, Steve Jobs, Mark Zuckerberg and Jeff Bezos could have advanced our world with the breakthrough products and services of Microsoft, Apple, Facebook, and Amazon respectively.

In addition, consider the added benefit of avoiding accidentally pitting yourself against the force of nature by heading in the wrong direction. Instead you can have a career propelled not by discipline or external enforcers but by internal biological drives to using and improving your most addictive and rewarding strengths and talents.

DOWNLOADING "BOOKS" IN ONE'S SAVANT DOMAIN

I speculated in Chapter 6, *Savant-Like Information Access by NonSavants*, that savants, prodigies, and other categories of nonsavants appear to externally source the organized "books" or "systems of information" relevant to their savant domain. It was as if they had checked a manual out of nature's library which contained only the factual and procedural information they needed for genius in their specific savant domain.

In the case of someone with multiple personality disorder, they accessed "personbooks" with the complete system of physical and personality traits and knowledge system for each of the personalities they exhibit. There is an example in Carrey's savant-domain career which suggests this same downloading of a "personbook" in his savant domain.

Carrey won a Golden Globe award for the biopic "Man on the Moon." Many in the know swear that Jim channeled comedian Andy Kaufman. His performance was incredibly accurate even though Jim had never met Kaufman. It is as if Carrey downloaded the entire "personbook" or system of Andy Kaufman's physicality and personality.

With no guile whatsoever, Jim was so into the role that he could only answer to the name "Andy" for the duration of filming. It actually would not register when he was called "Jim." Milos Forman, the director, claims he only met Jim Carrey twice during the shooting. Otherwise, he felt he was talking to Andy. He claims Jim woke up every morning as "Andy." [22]

Carrey felt that his role as Kaufman was not acting or impersonation but the result of a possession. "I don't feel like I made the film at all. I feel like Andy made the film." [23]

This download of relevant "books" or "systems of information" is something you can expect during savantflows in your own savant domain. These externally sourced information systems allow you to operate beyond your potential just as with savants. This is part of being grouped with relevant systems by nature's self-ordering librarian for mutually beneficial information-sharing.

This download of "books" or systems of information may also explain Oprah's brilliance as a preschooler in reciting, with full animation, the transformative sermons of mesmerizing preachers. She loved uplifting people so much that she too was in her savant-domain flow state where the magic happens.

> *My soul is not contained within the limits*
> *of my body. My body is contained within*
> *the limitlessness of my soul.* Jim Carrey

---

[22]   *Jim Carrey and Milos Forman talk about Man on the Moon Andy Kaufman and each other*, jimcarreyonline, published on Jun 30, 2009
https://www.youtube.com/watch?v=5RjnsSlt3Nc
[23]   Ian Crouch, "*Jim Carrey Ceases to Exist in "Jim & Andy: The Great Beyond*," November 17, 2017, The New Yorker

9

Oprah: An Uplifting Career

Oprah quotes on "calling" a.k.a. "savant domain:"

- *I've come to believe that each of us has a personal calling that's as unique as a fingerprint – and that the best way to succeed is to discover what you love and then find a way to offer it to others in the form of service, working hard, and also allowing the energy of the universe to lead you.*

- *Everybody has a calling. And your real job in life is to figure out as soon as possible what that is, who you were meant to be, and to begin to honor that in the best way possible for yourself.*

- *Your calling isn't something that somebody can tell you about. It's what you feel. It is the thing that gives you juice. The thing that you are supposed to do. And nobody can tell you what that is. You know it inside yourself.*

- *You've got to follow your passion. You've got to figure out what it is you love – who you really are. And have the courage to do that. I believe that the only courage anybody ever needs is the courage to follow your own dreams.*

- *There is no greater gift you can give or receive than to honor your calling. It's why you were born. And how you become most truly alive.*

- *The only courage you will need is the courage to live the life you are meant to."*

- *Embrace your uniqueness. You are different, your gift is special – own it and unapologetically share it with the world.*

- *The whole point of being alive is to evolve into the complete person you were intended to be.*

- *You know you are on the road to success if you would do your job, and not be paid for it.* [This is the *unpaid work theme* I mentioned in Chapter 3 which identifies your path to merging with the bioflow and accessing savant-level genius.]

As the above quotes illustrate, Oprah believed everyone has a "calling" and she encourages us to pursue ours just as she has followed her savant domain to achieve her success. "Calling" is a mild term for "savant domain." It does not capture the biological consequences of shifting into the peak states of savantflows or the extensions and upgrades from merging with the bioflow. These are the dynamics behind the externally sourced genius of Oprah's life right from childhood.

A Single Savant Domain from Childhood

Oprah demonstrated savant-like genius when she repeated powerful sermons she'd heard only once starting when she was just three and a half. She presented these sermons replete with all the emotion and animation of the original speaker. She was complying with her biological drives to repackage messages that were meaningful to her to uplift others – the beginnings of what became a life theme for her.

Oprah freely admits that she had no understanding of what she was saying but found the need to help people with the sermons irresistible. "I realized, from the time that I was a little girl, that my role is to inspire, encourage and uplift. I've been doing that since I was three years old, really. I want to let people see the light inside themselves."[24]

With sermon "books" of spontaneous knowledge downloading into her head at such a young age, it is obvious that Oprah's savant domain was innate, not learned. What was play or compelling as a child became paid play as an adult for all six of our superachievers. Honoring savant-domain drives releases biological benefits not available with any other formula.

One's natural growth path

However, those drives were also the reason she vacated positions of success three times in her career for risky opportunities of potentially less success but greater meaning. I'm referring to the below events:

a) leaving a successful hosting job to take a chance on owning her own "Oprah Winfrey Show" where she could pursue her own agendas;

b) changing the underlying format of the very successful "Oprah Winfrey Show" in the 1990s to do more good after failing to do so in two of her shows. She continued with this mission despite losing viewers; and then to

c) narrowing her success even further through launching her OWN cable network in 2011. However, she would now have greater freedom to uplift the masses with her personal approach.

As with all six superachievers, Oprah was driven by the intrinsic rewards of her work and growth path every day rather than the extrinsic rewards she ultimately achieved and to which so many aspire. If one complies with the bioflow, one will be led on a natural growth path which proceeds in two directions.

Because savanting is about expressing one's core essence at its maximum, growth will be an expansion by concentric circles around that core to an ever-widening impact on the world. Growth will also narrow to more precisely express one's essence. This is what we are seeing with each of the three risky career moves that Oprah made above.

We see this same narrowing when Bill Gates shifts from improving the world with the products of Microsoft to improving the world more directly through his very targeted mega-philanthropy. He too stepped down from a highly successful position for another of his own making for increased meaning, impact, and expression of his essence.

Oprah was true to a singular advance of her savant domain. From her Harvard commencement address in 2013, she shares the singularity of her savant domain. "The goal of my shows, my interviews, my business, my philanthropy, all of it, whatever ventures I might pursue, would be to make clear that what unites us is ultimately far more redeeming and compelling than anything that separates me."[25]

Oprah surrenders to the bioflow

As you might expect from someone operating at their maximum, a string of coincidences led Oprah to her life-changing experiences with the book (1982), movie (1985), and Broadway show (2005) entitled "The Color Purple." Oprah claims "The Color Purple" was a seminal moment in her life.

She became obsessed with this book from the moment she first learned of it. She read about it, bought it, and inhaled it in the same day. She then bought out the bookstore to give it away to others so they too might be uplifted by its message.[26]

The story helped Oprah to overcome the oppression, abuse, rape, poverty, beatings, discrimination, and neglect of her childhood and the many challenges of being female and African American while pursuing a career. It cleared her head and heart so she might better nurture and nourish others as she was biologically predisposed to do.

Alice Walker, the author, won the National Book Award and the Pulitzer Prize for Fiction for "The Color Purple." Oprah obviously has a gift for identifying talent and import. Have you noticed that Oprah serves as a conduit to so many others who facilitate her mission?

As a growth addict, she screens and selects the messages of authors and artists which can contribute to her mission to uplift, help, grow, and transform. She then packages and promotes them for mass impact. Remember preschool Oprah repackaging sermons or the famous Oprah's Book Club? And, Oprah has proven compelling in her mission no matter what medium she has chosen.

Winfrey said that, to this day, she has never been happier in her life than when she worked on "The Color Purple" film. When Oprah heard that Steven Spielberg was going to make a film of "The Color Purple" she became obsessed with the idea of acting in it. She claims she hadn't wanted anything so much in her life.

Yet, in the early 80s, Winfrey was just the weight-challenged host of a tiny local Chicago talk show. Oprah had never even acted before. She was so green that she thought she should look at the camera during takes because that is what she did as a TV host.

Yet Oprah wanted so badly to be part of the film's transformative story. She wanted the opportunity to further absorb the enlightenment inherent in its themes. She wanted to extend her channels for uplifting storytelling to an acting medium.

Winfrey overcame obstacles, adversity, and stiff competition to get her dream role as Sofia. In the process, she realized she had discovered a new way to achieve goals. Oprah revealed, "I learned the principle of surrender" from that experience.

In her 2014 interview with Christina Radish, Winfrey explained, "The principle of surrender is after you've done all you can do you have to release it. I have used that principle about a million times in my life. I realized that when you've done everything that you can do, when you've given it the best that you know how, you surrender it to that which is greater than yourself." Her theme song became "I Surrender All."[27]

Oprah fashions her advice in other terms. "Move with the flow. Don't fight the current. Resist nothing. Let life carry you. Don't try to carry it." "Follow your feelings. If it feels right, move forward. If it doesn't feel right, don't do it."

Her surrender is not a spiritual construct or a jolt of religious or new age wisdom as one might assume Oprah is implying. Rather, you'll come to see this surrender as compliance with the bioflow maximizing your system within the process of maximizing humanity. The bioflow forms a guidance system that has guided Oprah and our other superachievers to their greatest performance. With practice, you'll come to know the signposts of the guidance system in order to exploit it for your own goals.

People assume greatness comes from linearly pursuing one's goals. They will exert great control and discipline to push through every obstacle to adhere to a straight line to their goals. However, nature's bioflow is nonlinear. Therefore, when you partner with nature's maximizing machinery, your progress will be nonlinear.

You'll thus have to release yourself from demanding linear progression so that you can be taken to the right information at the right time for breakthroughs, coincidences, leaps, and facilitating events and people. This is Oprah's surrender.

With the savant-inspired internal-external partnering it is now possible to understand what nature's guidance system is up to. We don't have to have Oprah's *"unknowing surrender."* Rather, it is predictable. We can "know" what the biological machinery is trying to accomplish and comply with its goals in a way that supports achieving our own goals.

The bioflow is trying to maximize living systems including yours. The maximum of your system is a constant. How nature maximizes your system is a constant. You can know both from an examination of events in your past. Therefore, you can predict what kinds of goals and projects will and will not be supported in your future.

But more than this, we can capitalize on this predictability. We can help nature with its goals in order to better achieve our own. We can *"shrewdly surrender"* to capitalize on a predictable, "knowable" force that helps us achieve our goals.

Those who flow as life flows know they need no other force. Lao Tzu

To submit isn't to be forced. It's to yield to a force greater than your own, in order to become part of the whole. Dianna Hardy, Cry of The Wolf

*If you're willing to listen to, be guided by, that still
small voice that is the G.P.S. within yourself — to
find out what makes you come alive — you will be
more than okay. You will be happy ...*[28]
Oprah Winfrey

---

[24]   *Oprah Winfrey Talks Her Career, How The Color Purple Changed Her Life.
. . . and More,* Interview with Christina Radish, February 7, 2014 at the Santa
Barbara International Film Festival: SBIFF
http://collider.com/oprah-winfrey-the-butler-color-purple-interview/
[25]   *Winfrey's Commencement Address,* May 31, 2013 The Harvard Gazette
[26]   *Oprah Winfrey Talks Her Career, How The Color Purple Changed Her Life.
. . . and More,* Interview with Christina Radish, February 7, 2014
[27]   *Oprah Winfrey Talks Her Career, How The Color Purple Changed Her Life.
. . . and More,* Interview with Christina Radish, February 7, 2014
[28]   *Winfrey's Commencement Address,* May 31, 2013 The Harvard Gazette

10

Childhood Drives of Famous Founders

The founders of Microsoft, Apple, Facebook, and Amazon

We have examined the constellation of drives that have propelled Jim Carrey's life and career in his savant domain since he was a young boy. And we did the same for Oprah. Both taught us things about how to use savanting to partner with the bioflow. Now let's continue with our investigation using the lives of the four famous founders of Microsoft, Apple, Facebook, and Amazon.

As with Oprah and Carrey, the addictive play of their childhood also continued as the paid play of adulthood. They formed their companies around that play and that addiction. Their extraordinary success validates that this is the ideal formula for entrepreneurs to succeed. The four iconic founders worked at their maximum in tandem with nature's biostructures to do work to which they were biologically predisposed.

The companies of the four, therefore, emerged from the pull of their drives towards the ideal context for them to use and improve their most rewarding system of talents. They were pulled towards intrinsically rewarding activities daily which triggered serial savantflows.

They were *pulled* by addictive drives rather than having to be *pushed* by discipline to do tedious work. This is the true formula for their success which we may all emulate. This is the formula for biology-driven superachieving.

Steve Jobs, Apple co-founder, consumer engineer and hardware artist

Steve Jobs died on October 5, 2011 at the age of 56. Forbes ranked Steve as #34 in Forbes' "American Billionaires" (2011) up from #42 in 2010. With a net worth of $8.3 billion, Steve was ranked #110 in Forbes "World Billionaires" (2011). He ranked #17 in "Powerful People" (2010). At the time of his death, Steve Jobs' net worth was estimated at $10.2 billion.

In 2019, Forbes placed Laurene Powell Jobs, Steve Jobs' wife, at #54 in the "Billionaires" list. She had a net worth of almost $20 billion from the stakes in Apple and Disney which she inherited from her deceased husband.

Jobs had a net worth of more than a million dollars by 1978 when he was just 23 years old. That net worth had grown to $10 million by the next year and more than $250 million by the age of 25, according to many estimates.

His early fortune was based on the success of Apple personal computers, especially the Apple II. It made him one of the youngest people ever on Forbes' list of the richest people in the United States. What's more, he was part of a very tiny group of people under 30 to make the list with no inherited money.

Steve was an exceptional visionary. As a creative genius, he either created or totally transformed many big industries with his products and companies: personal computers (Apple II), graphical user interfaces (Macintosh), digital animation (Pixar), music hardware (the iPod), music distribution (iTunes), smartphones (the iPhone), and tablets (the iPad). He was a consumer engineer with the artistry to create products which people genuinely loved for their beauty and functionality.

From an early age, Jobs immersed himself in the small community of computer visionaries who, from the late 1960s and early 1970s onward, realized that a computer was far more than the calculating device implied by its name.

The childhood drives that guided the career of Jobs to such levels of success might be demonstrated by a story of the launch of his partnership with Apple co-founder, Steve Wozniak, as teenagers. Walter Isaacson's authorized biography of Steve Jobs describes an encounter between Jobs, Steve Wozniak, and Wozniak's father.[29]

Jerry Wozniak was a rocket scientist who tended to discount the merits of anyone who was not an engineer. During the exchange, Jerry aggressively told Jobs that he had not actually created anything and therefore did not deserve a 50 percent stake in the new business. Jobs, still a young teenager, began to cry.

He said he would walk away and let Steve Wozniak run the operation himself. But the younger Wozniak understood the synergy between Jobs and himself. He knew the company would need Jobs' entrepreneurial drive, vision, strategic thinking, and mesmerizing communications. Wozniak knew it was Jobs who could formulate ingenious consumer design to challenge his technology genius and then package their inventions for profit in the marketplace.

Indeed, it was Jobs who pioneered Apple's first marketing plan: "a computer for the rest of us" within a world of large corporate computers. Jobs focused Apple on products that addressed consumers' needs, feelings, and motivations. Wozniak says Apple probably never would have existed had it not been for Jobs' vision for selling the computers in consumer-focused packaging.

The host of products and services for which Apple is known and that have revolutionized the tech industry resulted from this commitment. The younger Wozniak was right.

Here are Jobs' own words, "I was lucky – I found what I loved to do early in life. Woz and I started Apple in my parents' garage when I was 20. We worked hard, and, in 10 years, Apple had grown from just the two of us in a garage into a $2 billion company with over 4000 employees." [30]

Before Jobs death in 2011, Apple said it had sold more than 300 million iPods, over 100 million iPhones, and more than 15 million iPad devices. Billions of songs had been sold from its iTunes Store. Even when Jobs was forced to leave Apple involuntarily, Jobs continued with the same consumer directions in his new company called NeXT, Inc. (and later NeXT Computer, Inc. and NeXT Software, Inc). He, in effect, continued with his savant domain in another context.[31]

Jobs never left his lifelong passion as a consumer engineer. He even studied art in his teens to better create compelling products that consumers loved. He was dedicated to advancing the world of technology to transform the lives of consumers. It was the *raison d'être* of his life.

Bill Gates, Microsoft co-founder, worldbuilder

The 2019 Forbes 400 list of "Billionaires" ranks Bill Gates as the second richest person in the world down from #1 for 18 of the past 24 years. He has a net worth of $96.5 billion. In 1999, his wealth topped $101 billion. Bill only has 1% of the shares of Microsoft remaining though he continues as a board member.

On June 27, 2008, Gates transitioned out of a day-to-day role in the company to spend more time on his global health and education work at the Bill & Melinda Gates Foundation. He served as chairman of the board until February 4, 2014.

Gates donated $35.8 billion worth of Microsoft shares to the Foundation which is now the largest private charitable foundation. The Gates have received numerous awards for their philanthropic work throughout the world.

Forbes' 2018 annual ranking of "The World's Most Powerful People" places Bill Gates at #7. "Time" magazine named Gates one of the most influential people of the 20th century.

A young Bill Gates envisioned a world in which everyone's life was improved by having access to a computer just as his own life had been. The personal computer powered by Microsoft software revolutionized our worlds of work and recreation. Gates infused Microsoft with a virtual monopoly on operating systems for PCs. Microsoft became an enormous multinational corporation as a result.

The famous software wizardry of Bill Gates was irresistible play that got him into trouble as a child until it got him into Microsoft and money as an adult. He loved what software allowed him to create and achieve.

But programming was only a tool for Bill's passion and creativity for business. And business was only a tool for his true domain as a worldbuilder populating new meaningful frontiers with the infrastructure necessary to improve the quality of life of humanity – of *individuals en masse*. Gates has always been passionate about helping people to grow and succeed – his employees, his customers, his partners, his donors, and the recipients of his philanthropy.

Gates' greatest missions are those which address the pivotal points of transformation for the people of the world. He may not have yet perfectly replaced Microsoft in that regard. However, there is no doubt he will continue to try.

Microsoft was pulling civilization into a new frontier and a transformed future. Bill is a gifted worldbuilder. However, the Gates' mega-philanthropy is, for the time-being, mainly addressing the flaws of civilization by opening the most meaningful channels for all who can help to indeed help. An incredible ambition.

However, I forecast that, in a role reversal, he'll *springboard* off of Jeff Bezos' Amazon approach to philanthropy or *leapfrog* it to shift back into his worldbuilding strength. Gates' mega-philanthropy infrastructure could be expanded by the same recruiting process he is currently using to create it.

Gates could then use these global channels to ensure our greatest talents, technology, and inventions received the money and support they need to direct human evolution beneficially.

More about Bezos' worldbuilding approach to philanthropy in the *Missions for Mankind* chapter and *leapfrogging* and *springboarding* in the chapter entitled *Environmental Scanning to fuel Breakthroughs*.

This would not only be more thrilling and more fun for Gates as an advance of his savant domain, but it would restart his money-making engine so that he had more to channel through his foundation and investments.

Gates' business acumen, creativity, and gift for negotiations and industry partnerships made Microsoft's less than stellar software the industry standard with a massive application ecosystem and nearly universal industry hardware support. Microsoft so completely dominated the personal computing industry that Apple nearly went out of business.

To gage Bill's creativity as inferior to that of Steve Jobs based on their respective hardware versus software product lines is to completely miss the real competition – Gates' strategic invention and innovation in creating a successful business and industry by linking together the necessary players and resources. He delivered Microsoft the market and then locked it in by unifying hardware manufacturers and consumers with operating systems and suites of software.

Bill's gift for identifying and laying down the foundations and infrastructure for new frontiers is now being applied to the mega-philanthropy "business." Therefore, he is continuing the creative advance of his savant domain today.

By age 11, Bill was insatiably delving into international affairs, business, and the nature of life, all of which became relevant when he co-founded Microsoft. By middle school, Gates had already committed to the idea of owning his own company. Bill and his childhood friend, Paul Allen, were ready to launch a company as teenagers but their parents wanted them to attend university. They both tried to comply but left Harvard before graduation.

Microsoft was an extension of natural drives in their childhoods. Bill's addiction to computers as a tool for business and creatively impacting the world began at age 13. He paid to use the single computer terminal at his school until his money ran out. Then Bill hacked into the computer to use it for free. This would become just the first of many times he was banned from a computer for hacking.

To get back into their good graces, Bill offered to debug the computer programs he had hacked to prevent others from following suit. In order to feed his addiction, his deal was to do this in exchange for computer time.

He later admitted that "it was hard to tear myself away from a machine at which I could so unambiguously demonstrate success." Bill's rare aptitude had been recognized while he was still in his teens. He began earning money from corporations as a programmer.

Gates sold his first software product to a school for about $4,000. At age 15, Bill and Paul sold their first joint product, "Traf-o-Data," for $20,000. While Gates was a prodigious programmer, it had already become evident that his flair for business was greater.

Their fascination with personal computing began in the summer of 1974 with a serendipitous "Popular Electronics" article on the Altair 8800 mini-computer kit. With great chutzpah reflective of his confidence in their talent, Gates contacted the company to proclaim that he and Paul were working on a BASIC software program that would run the Altair computer. They were not. But the company was interested so the two friends pulled it off. The program sold for $3,000.

In 1975, while still at Harvard, Bill and Paul formed the now famous Microsoft – a blend of their focus on "micro-computers" and "software" – to scale the frontiers of these two new industries. Bill was inspired by the potential to elevate the quality of life of everyone worldwide.

Bill's departure from Microsoft to join his wife at the Bill and Melinda Gates Foundation was not simply a matter of his wealth. It was an extension of this passion for elevating the quality of life *en masse* through high-growth, high-impact, international business, unprecedented technology, and eventually through the business of mega-philanthropy, another field which he pioneered.

Bill worked in compliance with his drives to use his strongest, most rewarding talents whether he was unpaid, paid, or philanthropically paying money out. As mentioned for Oprah, Bill had followed the two directions of growth that emerge naturally from savanting and the partnership with the bioflow orchestrating human evolution.

He had expanded by concentric circles the depth and impact of the creative expression of his core until his impact was felt globally. He then narrowed his focus to a dedication to improving the lives of those who needed it most by creatively generating the infrastructure and partnerships of his next frontier, the business of mega-philanthropy. Like Oprah, he left a lucrative position to risk more precisely expressing his core essence.

I have identified creativity as the re-combining of existing information systems to generate a new information system. This precisely describes the work of Bill Gates in his savant domain. He bought existing software and re-combined it to create new software. In the same way, he combined business entities to generate new industry infrastructure.

Similarly, he united mega-donors to eradicate diseases and other deficiencies in the world that governments were failing to address on their own. He continued to be dedicated to *improving the lives of individuals en masse* and he had the creativity for unifying world resources to do it.

This is the essence of the man. This is the channel which gives meaning to the strengths which created Microsoft's success. His vison, his negotiation skills, his ability to identify new frontiers and opportunities, and to design and recruit the resources and entities necessary to scale those frontiers and solidify them with new enduring infrastructure. Bill is gifted at recruiting people, talent, infrastructure, resources, and power to worldchanging causes.

Mark Zuckerberg, Facebook co-founder, worldbonder

Facebook.com has become the most popular and widely used social networking site behind Google. Facebook's market worth is about $541.5 billion. Mark still owns 15% of the company. He's ranked #8 on the Forbes' "Billionaires" list for 2019 with a net worth of $62.3 billion. He's #13 on their 2018 annual ranking of the "World's Most Powerful People." This is up from #22 in 2014. Mark has proclaimed his priority in 2019 is tackling social issues.

Zuckerberg is the world's youngest billionaire and one of the most talked about entrepreneurs in the business world. "Time" magazine named Zuckerberg "Person of the Year" in 2010, and Vanity Fair placed him at the top of their "New Establishment" list.

In May 2012, Facebook issued its initial public offering. It raised $16 billion. This was the biggest internet IPO in history. In 2013, Facebook made the Fortune 500 list for the first time. At the age of 28, Zuckerberg was the youngest CEO on the list. By January 2014, Facebook's market capitalization had risen to over $134 billion.

As with our other superachievers, Mark's focus is on the betterment of individuals *en masse*. Facebook is a continuation of Mark's drives to improve quality of life by building and strengthening each person's relationships. Since childhood, Zuckerberg's "work that is play" has been to connect and unify communities, tribes, families, and ultimately the planet. He is a "worldbonder."

And, as with our other iconic founders, Zuckerberg chose to build a company around his savant domain. For all of you wanting your own company, you'll come to know this is the ideal strategy for success.

The movie, "The Social Network," gives us a glimpse into the addictive play that engaged Zuckerberg's greatest talents and drives in the creation of Facebook. Mark was a brilliant computer programmer by age 12. He and his friends created computer games for the enjoyment of friends and family. He helped to create "Zucknet" to interconnect the computers of his family and their businesses so they could more easily communicate with each other. His passion for social networking had already begun in his childhood.

His social networking continued at Harvard. Mark built a program called "CourseMatch" to help students choose their classes based on the course selections of other users. He invented "Facemash" which compared the pictures of two students on campus and allowed users to vote on which one was more attractive. Community was created around a shared process and people.

Then Zuckerberg and his friends created a site called "The Facebook" that allowed users to create their own profiles, upload photos, and communicate with other users. He had discovered his obsession. As with Bill Gates and Paul Allen, Mark was too passionate and too impatient to advance his community-building savant domain to finish his Harvard degree.

> Jeff Bezos is said to be an intense, micromanaging
> individual who loves his work:
> *"I dance into the office every morning."*[32]

Jeff Bezos, Amazon founder, worldbuilder

In the Forbes' 2019 "Billionaires" list, Amazon.com founder and CEO Jeff Bezos is now number one with a net worth of $160 billion after a one-year gain of $78.5 billion. Forbes' 2018 annual ranking of "The World's Most Powerful People" places Jeff at #5.

As the founder and CEO of online global retailer, Amazon.com, Jeff Bezos is often considered to be the inventor and developer of e-commerce. Harvard Business Review ranked Bezos as the second-best CEO in the world. U.S. News & World Report identified Bezos as one of America's best leaders. "Time" magazine named Bezos its "Person of the Year" for 1999 and anointed him the "King of Cybercommerce."

Amazon.com launched in July 1995 from the garage of the Bezos' home in suburban Seattle, Washington. Almost overnight and with no press, Amazon changed the book-buying habits of the planet. Only two months after its launch, Amazon.com was selling $20,000 worth of books per week.

Jeff is a self-proclaimed "change junkie." From an early age, he was in a perpetual state of invention, creation, scaling new frontiers, learning the new, and penetrating new and unknown territories. His parents' garage looked like a science fair awash with his projects. His mother was forced to make frequent trips to RadioShack to keep up with her son's need for supplies.

This multi-projected garage is a forerunner of his experimenting modus operandi for running Amazon and the diverse interests of his career in evidence inside and outside of Amazon.

Bezos would seem not to have the drives to a singular savant domain as with the other careers we have been examining. This is not the case. Strategies, tactics, and investments which seem helter-skelter, actually are extremely focused.

A good way to not only understand Jeff but be able to predict his future actions is to accept that his addictive drives pull him to make history – and *"big history"* at that. *He is a worldbuilder –*

with all of the diversity which that pursuit entails. He is driven to do the unprecedented to advance humanity.

He is driven to build what has never existed before. He will always be pioneering, venturing, experimenting, and entrepreneuring *to better the quality of life of individuals en masse.*

But he has a very specific conduit of interest for developing his skills, experimenting with approaches, and making investments. *The colonization of space.* Suddenly a clear savant-domain pathway from Jeff's childhood to the present and to his future becomes evident. Follow the very distinct progression below to perceive the order in his seeming chaos.

1. The savant domain for Jeff Bezos is and always will be an extension of the worldbuilding books he read voraciously in childhood from science fiction writers such as Jules Verne, Isaac Asimov, and Robert Heinlein.

2. At an announcement event for Blue Origins, Jeff revealed the start of his passion for space: "Millions of people were inspired by the Apollo Program. I was five years old when I watched Apollo 11 unfold on television, and without any doubt it was a big contributor to my passions for science, engineering, and exploration. You don't get to choose your passions. Your passions choose you. For whatever reason, when I was 5 years old, Neil Armstrong stepped onto the moon. I was imprinted with his passion for space and for exploration."

3. In his high school valedictorian speech, Jeff confessed his "dream of saving humanity by creating permanent human colonies in orbiting space stations while turning the planet into an enormous nature preserve."

The 18-year-old Bezos said he "wanted to build space hotels, amusement parks and colonies for 2 million or 3 million people who would be in orbit." As a kid, Jeff never talked about being a spaceman. He wanted to be a "space entrepreneur."

4. While at university, Bezos was President of the Princeton chapter of the "Students for the Exploration and Development of Space."

5. One misstep on Bezos' path occurred when he attempted to follow his hero, theoretical physicist and cosmologist, Stephen Hawking, into space by pursuing a physics degree at Princeton University.

   Jeff was surrounded by gifted physicists at Princeton. While his marks were good, he knew he did not love the work as they did. It was not his "art." He had to work ten times harder to keep pace with the savants in his class.

   For the first time, he was not in his savant domain doing intrinsically rewarding activities as he had done since childhood. He was neither prodigy nor genius in the field that would help him to become a space entrepreneur.

   However, there was a new hero on the horizon. There was a new frontier to explore instead of his passion for Hawking's outer space. Bill Gates was making waves with the entrepreneurial explosion of Microsoft. Jeff had loved computers since grade 4. He was intrigued by anything that could be revolutionized by computers.

   Coincidentally for Bezos, Princeton had just begun to offer a degree in the new field of computer science. Jeff's addiction to invention, creativity, and breadth of impact had found a better home. He graduated with a 4.2 grade average earning a B.Sc.

for a double major for a tough degree in electrical engineering and computer science.

6. In 2000, Bezos founded his consumer spaceflight company, Blue Origin, to develop new technology for consumer spaceflight with the ultimate goal of establishing an enduring human presence beyond the Earth.

    Was Blue Origin an extension of Amazon's growing distribution network? Or was the global spread of Amazon and its diversification the preparation or dry run for colonization of space once the rockets began operating routinely?

    Most people would have assumed Amazon was primary. However, Jeff's savant domain would suggest that Amazon was subservient to the Blue Origin goal.

7. So how does one prepare for the colonization of space? Jeff's savant domain explains his decision as a top graduate from an Ivy League university to ignore all the offers from the big Fortune 500 companies. Instead he chose to make history by worldbuilding at a small global entrepreneurial startup.

    Bezos worked on Wall Street on the large computer networks that would ultimately let him make a global impact in his own company. These computer networks are always his foundational tool for his worldbuilding.

    Bezos first worked on building a network for international trade for a company known as Fitel. Jeff worked next on the large networks of Bankers Trust. Later he worked on internet-enabled business opportunities at D. E. Shaw & Co.

8. Jeff's need to be revolutionary and worldbuilding explains his risky decision to leave the security of a high-paying job on Wall

Street to move across the country to start an unprecedented e-commerce venture called Amazon.com using a little-known, unproven, and uncommercialized network of computers called the internet. Jeff needed to be worldbuilding on a planet-wide basis for "consumers" rather than "businesses" until he could begin colonizing space.

When he discovered that the web was growing at 2,300 percent per year, he recognized that *the internet was a once-in-a-generation phenomenon that no global-expansionist, no history-making pioneer, no worldbuilder* would want to miss. There was no other possibility for someone with his savant domain.

He knew instantly that this was his next step towards worldbuilding and colonizing space. Because he knew that he was on the path to his full creative expression there was no risk too great.

He also knew that coincidences and facilitating events would confirm his decision. And that, you will discover shortly, is exactly what happened. Since Amazon was the fastest route to the money and experience necessary to Blue Origin and his space colonization mission, it would be supported by the bioflow with coincidences and breakthroughs.

9. What do you do when you are ready to begin colonizing space but you are stuck here on Earth? What Bezos has done is increased the spread, depth, and diversification of Amazon and a multitude of other investments. If you look closely, you will see his investments are fleshing out what he would need to know for his space colonization. In the interim Jeff continues to expand his worldbuilding efforts on Earth.

As I alluded earlier, Jeff's savant domain may appear a little more complex than most, but I think you can see that it has, in fact, been rather singular in its focus. If Amazon disappeared tomorrow, one can predict the form of its eclectic replacement. Jeff's worldbuilding theme would continue.

Savant domain summary for five founders

Notice how the savant domain of each addresses their focus on bettering the life of the individual across a multitude of individuals. Uplifter Oprah does it with a teaching network through which she channels experts on various fronts. She loves both the sourcing of the information through her voracious reading and meetings with experts and its distribution through her interviews and storytelling. She is orchestrating a shared growth process.

Worldbuilder Bill Gates causes world transformation by creating networks of organizations, businesses, hardware manufacturers, products, software, donors, charities, government agencies, and such. He merged users globally by giving them a common "language" and products that would allow them to connect, share, and co-create globally.

The designs of artist and consumer engineer Steve Jobs bring joy to consumers and enhance their quality of life globally. Jobs advanced our world with an infusion of creativity and creations as an information technology entrepreneur, a microcomputer industry pioneer, and a computer-animation pioneer.

Worldbuilder Bill Gates causes world transformation by creating networks of organizations, businesses, hardware manufacturers, products, software, donors, charities, government agencies, and such. He merged users globally by giving them a common "language" and products that would allow them to connect, share, and co-create globally.

Worldbuilder Jeff Bezos elevates global infrastructure through large information-sharing computer networks and internet connections. Worldbonder Mark Zuckerberg does it by providing the infrastructure through which networks of people can be created, linked, extended, bonded, and channeled to support causes.

---

[29]   Walter Isaacson, *Steve Jobs*, October 24, 2011, Simon & Schuster
[30]   Steve Jobs, Commencement address on June 12, 2005, Stanford News
https://news.stanford.edu/2005/06/14/jobs-061505/
[31]   Jason Fell and Teri Evans, Remembering Apple's Steve Jobs, October 6, 2011, Entrepreneur.com on NBCnews.com
http://www.nbcnews.com/id/44834372/ns/business-small_business/t/remembering-apples-steve-jobs/#.XTpHont7k_U
https://www.entrepreneur.com/article/220492
[32]   Adam Lashinsky, Bezos Prime, March 24, 2016, Fortune Magazine

11

Intrinsic not Extrinsic Rewards

*I hope everybody could get rich and famous and will
have everything they ever dreamed of, so they will
know that it's not the answer.*   Jim Carrey

At its very foundation, savanting provokes one to do the work or creative expression of one's essence for which one is biologically predisposed. It capitalizes on positive biofeedback mechanisms which evolution has selected for installation over generations to entice us to function at our maximum for survival purposes.

When we do this, the mechanisms, resources, information, and power of the bioflow and all the living systems it orchestrates extend our capabilities to take us to a new more gratifying level of peak operation. Our six superachievers have lived lives in compliance with this biological wiring.

A common theme in all their careers is that the *extrinsic rewards* that mark their success, and to which so many aspire, were never pursued. Money, fame, security, and such were never their daily drivers. None of the six stopped working because they had enough money to do so. Larry Page, the co-founder of the enormously successful Google, reinforces the point, "If we were motivated by money, we would have sold the company a long time ago and ended up on a beach."

Rather, each was captivated by activities in their savant domain at an early age. They were pulled to action by rewards intrinsic to the projects they were passionate about doing rather than the extrinsic rewards which their work eventually attracted. Repeatedly they demonstrated that it was not the pursuit of money, fame, security, and such which resulted in their success.

Bill Gates

On November 1, 2013, Richard Waters wrote in the Financial Times that "through the stroke of pen on cheque book, Gates probably now has the power to affect the lives and well-being of a larger number of his fellow humans than any other private individual in history."

During his philanthropy years, Bill Gates has dedicated himself to missions to prevent childhood deaths, improve education, improve health and fight poverty in developing countries, tackle malaria, and pay for vaccination drives against infectious diseases. He is intent on the eradication of a disease that has blighted an untold number of lives – polio.

Despite this anomaly to public perception, most people continue to assume that, because Gates earned so much money, it must have been his goal throughout his career. Each of our six superachievers will deny this pursuit. In fact, the five founders would even deny that they followed strategic plans to arrive at the current form of their respective companies. Rather they advanced opportunistically with the bioflow.

Those aspiring to what Bill Gates has achieved will never reach that status by seeking it directly. No one has the discipline to do work they dislike for the long hours every day for decades for which Bill Gates is known. Bill loved what he did.

Gates was propelled ahead by self-created contexts in which his strongest most rewarding talents and drives would be engaged every day in meaningful intrinsically rewarding tasks – tasks which he could not resist doing on into the night without food or sleep. What makes the tasks intrinsically rewarding is the addictive biochemistry emerging from them. Gates' approach was organic and opportunistic in partnership with the evolutionary directions of the bioflow.

We can trace the theme of Gates' intrinsically rewarding activities right back to his childhood and we can predict what he will pursue in the future from a projection of that same theme. This is because his biological drives remain the same. He has remained biologically maximized and attached to the bioflow since childhood.

As you have already learned, the way to determine one's ideal context is to examine patterns of events triggering savantflows and support from the bioflow in one's past for themes which can predict the recurrence of those events in the future. This is one's savant formula for living a biologically maximized life.

Bill is driven by a thirst for new knowledge, new learning, new growth, new frontiers, new skills, new creations, and new levels of achievement. He creates contexts in which his most compelling constellation of rewarding drives could be meaningfully engaged in savantflows.

Gates is a worldbuilding achievement junkie – a speed zealot seeking the highs of the next execution, the next, and the next in his territory of meaning. He harnesses his passion for two tools – computers and business – to accelerate his progress and amplify his achievements.

However, his go-to execution accelerator is his creative genius for re-combining existing entities throughout his life to generate the unprecedented – software programs, businesses, organizations, industries, OED computer manufacturers, philanthropists, charitable organizations, governments, and so on.

This is a brilliant way to speed the execution he was craving. Through this re-combining process, Gates has laid down infrastructures that advanced business, his industries, new frontiers, civilization, and raised the quality of life for humanity. This is one of his intrinsically rewarding activities to which he is drawn.

You can see why this addiction could drive the success of Microsoft and philanthropy. At each opportunity or "decisionpoint," Bill puzzled through what could be re-combined to short-circuit the requirements to achieve this goal and the next and the next. This was his creative genius. And this was the thrill of the life he led and continues to lead.

Bill, then, was addicted to the thrill of *breakthrough-by-breakthrough execution* just as we saw with Bezos. They were both execution creatives. The work Gates has to do daily to accomplish these goals is its own reward. It is intrinsically rewarding work of perpetual invention. It was the pursuit of the next execution high and the next that built Microsoft not some ambition to a strategically sound business plan.

There was never a big plan as to what Microsoft would become and a striving to make it happen. There was instead the deal, the decision, or the opportunity right now that was invoking savantflows and the magic of the bioflow. The bioflow directed the evolution of Microsoft so that all the "decisionpoints" became a cumulative advance to our world.

The bioflow enables nonvisionaries to operate as if they have vision. All Bill needed to do was what he was passionate about each moment and re-combine the information systems that the bioflow had gathered at each "decisionpoint."

Some speculate that it was Bill's upbringing in a realm in which competition and winning were valued that trained him to be hard-driving and ambitious. This then is what people think they have to emulate to achieve Gates' success.

Instead it was biology. Think of the pull of the deal to a dealmaker biologically predisposed to it by emotional highs. Bill has been compliant with his biological strengths and dispositions since childhood. He hasn't separated from immersion in the bioflow. It was his biochemistry pulling him to his intrinsically rewarding dealmaking work not the discipline of teachings to be competitive. The formula for success shared by all six superachievers is doing the work that expresses their essence.

Steve Jobs

Steve Jobs once said, "You know, my main reaction to this money thing is that it's humorous, all the attention to it, because it's hardly the most insightful or valuable thing that's happened to me." Knowing this, would it surprise you to learn that when Steve Jobs rejoined Apple in 1997 after being let go from the company in 1985, he set his salary at just $1 according to a Securities and Exchange Commission filing?

Jobs reinforces the idea in his 1995 interview with Robert X. Cringley for the PBS documentary, "Triumph of the Nerds:" "I was worth over a million dollars when I was 23. And over ten million dollars when I was 24, and over a hundred million dollars when I was 25. And you know, it wasn't that important, because I never did it for the money . . . . The most important thing was the company, the people, the products we were making. And what we were going to enable people to do with these products. So I didn't think about the money a great deal."

In 2005, Steve Jobs gave the Commencement Address to those graduating from Stanford University. He revealed his true motivation: "I'm convinced that the only thing that kept me going was that I loved what I did. You've got to find what you love. If you haven't found it yet, keep looking. Don't settle. As with all matters of the heart, you'll know when you find it. And, like any great relationship, it just gets better and better as the years roll on."

On another occasion he said, "Your work is going to fill a large part of your life, and the only way to be truly satisfied is to do what you believe is great work. And the only way to do great work is to love what you do."

Mark Zuckerberg

Money was also not Mark Zuckerberg's driving force. Mark was committed to changing the world. Mark's proclaimed priority in 2019 is resolving social issues. Mark and his wife, Priscilla Chan, have pledged to give away 99% of their Facebook stake over their lifetimes.

When Zuckerberg launched Facebook, there was not even an identified way to earn money on the horizon. Yet he kept on with his mission of connecting people from Harvard to other universities, to high schools, and then beyond to the public at large. Mark has turned down millions and even billions of dollars from those wanting to buy Facebook or other things he has developed. He is doing the work that he wants to do and it has nothing to do with making money. However, because he and his team do it so well, he cannot help but attract wealth.

Jeff Bezos

In 2013, "Business Insider" listed Jeff Bezos' salary as only $14,000, little more than the average Facebook intern. In 2014, "Salary.com" lists a salary of only $81,840 for Jeff from his role of chief executive officer and director at Amazon.com Inc.

12

Missions for Mankind

*Self-actualizing people have a deep feeling of
identification, sympathy, and affection for human
beings in general. They feel kinship and connection
as if all people were members of a single family.*

Abraham Maslow, the American psychologist and
philosopher who coined the term "self-actualization."

The four successful companies of the iconic founders –
Amazon, Apple, Microsoft, and Facebook – are all
coincidentally dedicated to improving the lives of
individuals. Specifically, bettering the lives of individuals *en masse*.
Separate from their corporate philanthropy programs, their actual
products and services benefit humanity and catalyze its advance.
The missions of Jim Carrey and Oprah have a similar focus.

A philanthropic bent is not necessary to pursue serial
savantflows within one's savant domain. It is not a requirement of
the science behind savanting. However, *all savant domains will
eventually lead to contribution to the advance of humanity*. This is
because experiencing savantflows will connect you to the bioflow
that is maximizing, adapting, and evolving humanity. The bioflow
is dedicated to maximizing the individual and the species
synergistically. Therefore, selfishly pursuing one's own self-

actualization will lead to self-transcendent purposes which help others.

Also partnering with the forces behind the evolutionary advance of humanity is how the famous founders generated products ahead of the market. The bioflow has some predictable constants on which one may capitalize.

For example, it is always pressuring to unify humanity as a cohesive system. Any products or services which catalyze this unification will earn bioflow support – communication devices and products, for example, such as those from Apple and Microsoft. Or social and software networks such as from Facebook. Or the sharing of the knowledge and teachings of today's thinkers, writers, inventors, and teachers globally such as through Amazon.

Steve Jobs Mission

Steve Jobs was dedicated to bettering the lives of consumers. He was a committed "consumer engineer." From the launch of Apple with Steve Wozniak from a garage to his death, this was his singular focus. This is what defined meaning and direction for him. He was driven to change the world for the better. Apple's first marketing plan was "a computer for the rest of us" amid a world of large corporate computers.

Jobs infused his employees with an almost evangelical mission to help the people of the world. Some joked that it felt almost like projects were a mission from God. For Jobs, this was not about formulating a great mission statement. This is what drove him biologically and spiritually.

He cared more about excellence, achievement, and contribution than money. I think the ultimate testament to Jobs nonmonetary motivation is Apple's continuous commitment to quality over quantity from the beginning.

The people who are crazy enough to think they can
change the world are the ones who do. Steve Jobs

Bill Gates Mission

In Gates' own words, "When Paul Allen and I started Microsoft over 30 years ago, we had big dreams about software. We had dreams about the impact it could have. We talked about a computer on every desk and in every home. It's been amazing to see so much of that dream become a reality and touch so many lives. I never imagined what an incredible and important company would spring from those original ideas."[33] "I was lucky to be involved and get to contribute to something that was important, which is empowering people with software."

Bill visualized a personal computer in every home long before the means for achieving that goal was even on the horizon and long before we knew we each wanted one. He routinely concentrated on how lives could be improved with these personal computers and adjusted his software offerings accordingly.

As with the other founders, Bill had the typical drives of those complying with the bioflow – elevating the lives of individuals *en masse. A bidirectional nonlinear growth path is pressured by the bioflow: the expansion of one's impact by concentric circles around one's core essence while narrowing one to more precisely do the work for which one is biologically predisposed.*

In 1997, the bioflow orchestrated a dramatic narrowing in Bill's savant domain. As was the case with Oprah, Bill took considerable risk to comply with the savanting growth path. Gates had a pivotal, life-changing Aha! moment in Africa in 1997 when a heartbreaking event turned him to philanthropy. In an interview with Charlie Rose, Gates told the story:

"Well, the idea that a computer was relevant to the problems they were dealing with, where getting enough food, having decent health, getting any electricity, a reasonable place to live, it was pretty clear to me that, hey, I love this computer, and I thought it was neat and kids should have access, but they had to rig up a special generator so I could do this one demo.

"And they borrowed this generator. It wasn't going to be there when I left. So the idea that there was a hierarchy of needs . . . . While still believing in digital empowerment, that was not at the top of the list. That was pretty eye-opening for me."[34]

Bill stepped down as CEO of Microsoft in January 2000, three years later. He joined his wife and family members working at the Bill & Melinda Gates Foundation to more directly, more impactfully, and more meaningfully better the lives of individuals *en masse*.

The confirmation of Bill's true goal is captured in the mission of the Bill & Melinda Gates Foundation: "to remove the biggest barriers that prevent people from making the most of their lives by making bets on promising solutions that governments and businesses either can't afford to make or can't risk making given their stakeholders."

To pursue this goal, Bill applied his gift for international business and for inventing and structuring new territories to the upgrade of the field of mega-philanthropy.

In Bill's own words, he viewed his move to the Foundation as a continuation of his savant domain, "Effective philanthropy requires a lot of time and creativity – the same kind of focus and skills that building a business requires." "I believe the returns on investment in the poor are just as exciting as successes achieved in the business arena, and they are even more meaningful!"

We are seeing smarter philanthropy, more philanthropy, and that's true worldwide. So it's kind of a movement that has a lot of accomplishments, even though as a percentage of the economy, it's still only a few per cent.   Bill Gates

This [philanthropy] work is even more fascinating. It requires us to think harder about how we build partnerships, who we get behind. And yet we get to see progress that in some ways is even more profound than the great advances that digital technology has provided.   Bill Gates

Mark Zuckerberg Mission

In an August 2013 article by Mark Zuckerberg,[35] he asks in its title, "Is Connectivity a Human Right?" In the article, his answer is decidedly "Yes!" He believes "it is one of the greatest challenges of our generation." He explains and offers some strategies to solve the lack of internet connectivity in many areas of the world.

He points out that "Facebook was not originally created to be a company. It was built to accomplish a social mission – to make the world more open and connected."[36] This was Zuckerberg's opening to his statement of intent as the company held an IPO announcement.

Mark has used the social networking of Facebook as his means for unifying humanity. In 2008, his mission was phrased, "Facebook helps you connect and share with the people in your life." In 2013, "Facebook's mission is to give people the power to share and make the world more open and connected."

"There is a huge need and a huge opportunity to get everyone in the world connected, to give everyone a voice and to help transform society for the future. The scale of the technology and infrastructure that must be built is unprecedented, and we believe this is the most important problem we can focus on."

However, the expansions in consciousness from Zuckerberg's repeated savantflows was clearer from Facebook's 2012 IPO filing: "By simply making communication more efficient, [Facebook] led to a complete transformation of many important parts of society. [Facebook] gave more people a voice. [It] encouraged progress. [It] changed the way society was organized. [It] brought us closer together . . . .

"Facebook aspires to build the services that give people the power to share and help them once again transform many of our core institutions and industries . . . . Personal relationships are the fundamental unit of our society. Relationships are how we discover new ideas, understand our world and ultimately derive long-term happiness . . . . By helping people form these connections, we hope to rewire the way people spread and consume information."

Mark's focus continues to be to connect and unify communities, tribes, families, and ultimately the planet. It is significant that his wealth, fame, and power are byproducts of a social mission generously offered with no intent for garnering them.

> *Our society has an obligation to invest now to*
> *improve the lives of all those coming into this world,*
> *not just those already here.*   Mark Zuckerberg

Jeff Bezos Mission

The Amazon name derives from the symbolism of the earth's biggest river for the provision of the earth's biggest selection. Jeff's Amazon mission expanded from the "Earth's biggest bookstore" to the "Earth's biggest anything store" and then beyond retailing planet-wide to a future of retailing in space.

Jeff began taking action on this latest mission with the establishment of Blue Origin in 2000. This is an aerospace company seeking to develop technologies to provide the general public with the opportunity for spaceflight. Its mission is to establish an enduring human presence beyond Earth to solve major issues which humanity must face if we stay on the planet.

Jeff has been studying worldbuilding through science fiction books since his childhood. He will no doubt be ready for the worldbuilding we need in our communities in space. His need to perpetually scale new frontiers and his need to unify and heal humanity will make him the perfect "space entrepreneur" for all of us on planet Earth.

Jeff Bezos and Mark Zuckerberg are revolutionizing philanthropy by commercializing social missions. Jane Wales, CEO of the Global Philanthropy Forum says, "I think [Jeff Bezos'] activities to date suggest he looks at some of his business investments as opportunities to advance social change."

Bezos seems dedicated to furthering human progress through investment in for-profit companies. His leadership in this regard will shift how the world's wealthiest think about philanthropy.

Jeff's strategy for business investments to double as forms of social change was evident in his buying "The Washington Post" in 2013 and Whole Foods in 2017. His 2018 twitter call for short-term projects for lasting social change is a break in the preponderance of long-term strategies of many philanthropic foundations including those of his family and that of Bill Gates.

Missions from Expanded Consciousness

The missions of each of our four famous founders are not only directed by the bioflow. They are also informed by their view of the world from their bouts of expanded consciousness and altered awareness during decades of savantflows. As savantflows become deeper and more frequent, one's consciousness can even expand to become one with everything.

Unity consciousness, cosmic consciousness, and enlightenment become possible. Serial savantflows will trigger expansions of consciousness far beyond and far faster than what any spiritual disciplines could achieve. When your consciousness expands, one can see the interconnectedness, patterns, and trends more easily.

This expanded perspective is reflected in the mission statements of our four founders, their focus, what drives them, and eventually their contributions to humanity beyond the work of their companies. A global or planetary perspective has become their norm.

Cascading functionality upgrades

Repetitive experiences of savant-domain flow states will also launch accelerated growth in functionality and metaskills. One must be stretched beyond one's current capabilities in order for an activity to incite a flow state. Therefore, the six have not only operated with peak performance for decades but also peak growth as a way of life. With every flow state, they have increased their baseline functionality and level of performance.

In addition, with greater access to information and creativity in serial savantflows as a way of life, they achieve creations and innovations faster than competitors.

Now compare how much of your life you've spent in flow state around using and improving your best talents. Even if your capabilities were equal to these icons at birth, can you see how they could outperform you over their respective lifetimes?

Expansions in consciousness cause a chain reaction. Cognitive capabilities increase. Upgrades occur in conceptual skills, systems thinking, relational thinking, big-picture thinking, pattern recognition; the use of models, theories, and inferences; and the abilities for creative and opportunistic problem-solving, adaptivity, and inventiveness.

The "book" or "system" downloads of knowledge and skills will increase in frequency and size as savantflows deepen. Your flashes of genius and breakthroughs will become larger, more frequent, and more profound over time. Again, your performance baseline is elevated.

Imagine if all this increased skill and capability is singularly directed to your savant domain rather than dispersed and dissipated among many missions, interests, and fields. How much more could you accomplish as you pass through frontier after frontier on the same path? How much more could you attain if you had breakthrough building on breakthrough building on breakthrough?

This is how our four famous founders became worldchangers and worldbuilders. This is how you will make your greatest contribution to the advance of humanity while doing your most gratifying work and garnering your greatest intrinsic and extrinsic rewards.

You'll discover evidence of all this emerging over the lifetimes of our four founders. This is what will happen to you as well as soon as you begin a savantflow-based life. The formula is consistent, predictable, and replicable. Your goals and impact will upgrade along with your development of new capabilities, skills, and metacompetencies.

You will be expanding the creative expression of your core essence by concentric circles while narrowing to more precisely express that essence just as we saw with Bill Gates' nonretirement to mega-philanthropy and Oprah's risky career advances.

---

[33] Claudine Beaumont, *Bill Gates's dream: A computer in every home*, 27 Jun 2008. The Telegraph, Technology,
https://www.telegraph.co.uk/technology/3357701/Bill-Gatess-dream-A-computer-in-every-home.html
[34] Interview with Charlie Rose, *Bill and Melinda Gates on Philanthropy*, Published on Jan 21, 2015,
https://www.youtube.com/watch?v=3sucEddzDwY&feature=youtu.be
[35] Mark Zuckerberg "*Is Connectivity a Human Right,*" August 2013,
https://www.facebook.com/isconnectivityahumanright
[36] Mark Zuckerberg, Facebook's statement of intent re an IPO announcement, February 1, 2012, The Guardian
https://www.theguardian.com/technology/2012/feb/01/facebook-letter-mark-zuckerberg-text

13

Signs of Savantflows

S usan K. Perry, PhD affirms in her book, "Writing in Flow," that "flow is not a state of 'no mind' or meditativeness as such." "I don't believe that when you get into a creative place, you're giving up thinking," she says. "You're super-thinking – better and with more parts of your mind than you do normally."[37]

Flow happens, Perry suggests, "when our mind or body is voluntarily stretched to its limit." Is there evidence that our icons experienced the serial savantflows that are foundational to savanting?

Savanting's specialized subset of flow – savant-domain flow or savantflow – increases our experience of the externally sourced information behind the genius of savants. Savantflow brain and savant brain have similar capabilities with respect to the brain gatekeeper function for selective information access. We need this selective access to prevent overwhelm but, more importantly, so we have prioritized information for our survival.

For savants and nonsavants, only information relevant to one's savant domain enters awareness in certain states of consciousness. But the valve for accessing that information is wide open so that whole "books" or systems of information are accessible. This means that, for nonsavants, one has massive amounts of information relevant to the activity which incited one's savantflow. This is fuel for creativity.

Creativity is the re-combining of existing information systems to generate a novel information system. Therefore, in savantflow, one experiences a dramatic increase in quantum leaps in understanding such as breakthroughs, innovations, inventions, epiphanies, flashes of genius, and creative inspirations.

Since our internal maximizing machinery is linked to the bioflow maximizing machinery, the same quantum leaps in information from creativity occur outside in our reality as well. You can expect clusters of coincidences catapulting you ahead on the goals of your current savantflow activity.

Also, there will be external information events supporting your activity such as models for achieving your goal or facilitating people and events.

This is the same information access as breakthroughs and epiphanies. However, either the gatekeeper prevented the spontaneous inflow or it was more adaptive for the bioflow to present the model externally through a book, a periodical, a television show, or some person or event, for example.

Now think about the incredible accomplishments of our four famous founders. You are about to discover that their lives are replete with evidence of serial savantflows within their savant domains stretching back to their childhoods. Imagine how advanced they would have become after a lifetime of growth.

Programmer "hack mode"

All four founders had computer, internet, and software work in their childhood or early careers. Computer programming is particularly compelling for inciting flow states in general. Colloquially, these states are called "hack mode" which is often defined as "a Zen-like state of total focus." These flow states are so captivating that many programmers blissfully program all night and forget to eat or sleep. Imagine how much they could accomplish in a short period of time.

These states are so addictive that they not only became the "paid play" of our four founders but fostered an industry of computer and video games. These games allowed nonprogrammers to experience the same state of total engagement that was routine for programmers. Who has not willingly spent hours gaming no matter how hard one had to work?

For all intents and purposes, these hack-mode events were savantflows and all of our icons experienced them. "Gates would be in the middle of a line of code when he'd gradually tilt forward until his nose touched the keyboard," Microsoft co-founder Paul Allen revealed.

"After dozing an hour or two, he'd open his eyes, squint at the screen, blink twice, and resume precisely where he'd left off – a prodigious feat of concentration."[38]

Bill's programming addiction is reflected in his quote: "It was hard to tear myself away from a machine at which I could so unambiguously demonstrate success." Even as head of Microsoft, Bill was often discovered asleep at his work by those arriving in the morning.

Jeff Bezos is known to have kept a sleeping bag in his offices on Wall Street where programming was an important part of his work. And he was definitely known for his flow states. In Montessori preschool, teachers said "the boy became so engrossed in whatever he was doing that they had to pick his chair up, with him still in it, and move it to the next activity."[39]

Childhood friend Joshua Weinstein revealed, "He was excruciatingly focused. Not like mad-scientist focused, but he was capable of really focusing, in a crazy way, on certain things. He was extremely disciplined, which is how he is able to do all these things."[40]

That brings up another point. All four were labeled "workaholics." I disagree. "Playaholics" might be more appropriate. They were addicted to long hours of this "work" because it was fun and rewarding and kept them in biochemically addictive flow states where accelerated growth, creativity, and achievement were magnetically compelling.

To others not in their savant domain, this number of hours of work would make the classification of "workaholic" applicable. Not for these four, nor for Jim Carrey or Oprah for that matter. They were benefiting from savantflows which rejuvenate mind, body, and spirit.

The body's biochemistry would shut off the addictions and biological and psychological rewards of savantflow when it was not advantageous. Evolution would not have favored mechanisms which damaged us. Obviously, Gates' savantflows automatically shut off when it was time for him to sleep "nose to keyboard."

Jeff has embraced "work-life harmony" at Amazon over "work-life balance."[41] Actors frequently experience flow state so we can assume that Jim Carrey and Oprah both routinely experienced savant-domain flow states.

There is another key commonality in all savant-domain careers that we have not yet explored in the lives of our four iconic founders. All of them advanced their savant domains with creativity, innovation, breakthroughs, and flashes of genius. Nature's bio-machinery is geared to maximize the system of humanity. Therefore, all the component systems are advanced at the same time.

Consequently, one only needs to remain integrated with this bioflow as it advances one's savant domain to provide the kind of *global metamorphosis* orchestrated by our four entrepreneurs. The magic driving worldchanging breakthroughs and creations is the most pivotal element of the surprising savant-inspired protocol behind superachieving.

---

[37]   Susan K. Perry, *Writing in Flow: Keys to Enhanced Creativity*, May 1, 1999

[38]   Walter Isaacson, Dawn of a Revolution, September 20, 2013, the Harvard Gazette, https://news.harvard.edu/gazette/story/2013/09/dawn-of-a-revolution/

[39]   Jonathan Wai, *The Everything Kid - Even as a child, Jeff Bezos was a data-obsessed, workaholic genius*, January 3, 2014, Research Scientist, Duke University
https://qz.com/163262/even-as-a-child-jeff-bezos-was-a-data-obsessed-workaholic-genius/

[40]   Brad Stone, *The Everything Store: Jeff Bezos and the Age of Amazon*, August 12, 2014

[41]   Sarah Berger, Jeff Bezos doesn't like the idea of 'work-life balance' — here's what he swears by instead, cnbc.com Entrepreneurs, August 9 2018
https://www.cnbc.com/2018/08/09/what-jeff-bezos-does-instead-of-work-life-balance.html

IV

WORLDCHANGING BREAKTHROUGHS
the founders of Microsoft, Apple,
Facebook, and Amazon

Chapters

14

Creativity and Creations

All humans are entrepreneurs not because they
should start companies but because the will to create
is encoded in human DNA.
Reid Hoffman, Co-Founder, LinkedIn

The need for creativity in our fast-changing world is increasing. Creativity tops nearly every list of necessary skills ever produced by the Partnership for 21st Century Skills. This is a collection of 250 researchers at 60 institutions committed to collaborating with school systems and communities to realize the power and promise of 21st century learning.[42]

According to a 2010 global CEO study conducted by IBM of 1500 top executives in 60 countries, creativity was selected as the most crucial factor for future success.[43] Yet we still do not have consistency and predictability in being able to train people to be more creative. The increase in creativity during flow state is changing that.

Teresa Amabile is the Edsel Bryant Ford Professor of Business Administration and a Director of Research at Harvard Business School. Amabile discovered that not only are people more creative in flow, they also report being more creative the day after a flow state. This suggests that flow doesn't just heighten creativity in the moment. It heightens it long-term. Being in flow can train one to be more creative.[44]

Flow then is a serious solution to the world's creativity challenge. Instead of training people to be creative, one can train them to get into flow state and the changes in neurobiology will launch enhanced creativity. The addictiveness that evolution has built into both flow and creativity entice us to repeat the experience. The result is long-term creativity.

Now consider that all our superachievers have been in serial savantflows since childhood. Whether they were born creatives or noncreatives, significantly more creativity is going to emerge from their careers than most.

Therefore, it's no surprise that each of the four founders brought "the new" into existence. They are all entrepreneurial worldchangers. Apple, Microsoft, Facebook, and Amazon were all unprecedented entities launching new fields into being. Jobs and Gates were pioneers of the microcomputer revolution on the hardware and software sides, respectively. In fact, Jobs is said to have revolutionized six industries: personal computers, animated movies, music, phones, tablet computing, and digital publishing.

Through hundreds and eventually thousands of inventions and innovations, Mark Zuckerberg developed the means to attract billions of people to connect on Facebook. As a computer programming genius, internet entrepreneur, and social change advocate, he discovered how to more successfully commercialize social networking than his competitors. He has changed the interconnectivity of the world to unify the human race. Jeff Bezos is considered to be the inventor and lead innovator of e-commerce. All four have demonstrated continuous creativity to advance their respective savant domains.

Biological Immersion

Each operated at their maximum in their personal savant domain. This goes beyond simply applying one's talents to the maximum. It is about achieving an immersion so that one's capabilities are extended by other biological systems and mechanisms externally.

It is about conscripting the creativity fueling the adaptation and advance of human evolution to put you at the forefront of your field of genius. New routes to creativity, innovation, invention, and entrepreneurialism are available even to the noncreative when you are immersed into nature's creative engine.

How you operate and how much you can achieve all change when you shift to a paradigm in which you are extended by nature's bio-machinery. By examining the lives of our four superachievers, you will learn what is possible and how to operate in this new paradigm. You will see how superachievers cultivate the breakthroughs and creations which have changed our world.

The man who produces an idea in any field of
rational endeavor – the man who discovers new
knowledge – is the permanent benefactor of
humanity. Ayn Rand

Creativity: re-combine the existing to generate the new

The essence of creativity for nature's adaptation and advance of living systems is achieved by blending existing information systems to create novel systems which solve challenges to survival. Think of our reproductive process, for example. Two existing systems of genetic material combine to generate a new original human system.

But more than this, evolution advances by leaps or breakthroughs. There is no gradual linear process that could ever explain the evolution of a human eye, for example. Rather, it is more likely that existing successful eye structures were re-combined to create a new one adaptive for humans. You will see this *creational information synthesis* behind each of the inventions and accomplishments for which our four founders became known.

Continuous creation is a running theme throughout their careers. It will also become your way of life when you immerse yourself in addictive play in your savant domain. You'll come to routinely and continuously scan your domain for the information pieces to be blended to produce new creative breakthroughs and leaps.

This will be aided by the fact that nature's "librarian" routinely groups living systems – including compliant human beings – which are mutually beneficial or symbiotic. This is part of nature's self-organizing process dedicated to improving the survival of living systems. Exploiting these "synergy groupings" – this dynamic external order – will become the new pastime for all achievement junkies seeking breakthroughs and inventions. There is an order in this world that can be proactively exploited to routinely and rapidly generate breakthroughs.

> *We're here to put a dent in the universe. Otherwise why else even be here?*   Steve Jobs

Your drives merge with nature's drives

When you are in your savant domain, you have a completely different relationship with the events and information systems in your reality. Rather than the disorder of chaotic events, you find events synergistic with your purpose propelling you forward.

The Irish blessing, "May the road rise up to meet you," comes to fruition. You are operating in keeping with your biological predisposition in harmony with nature's intent. *Your drives are merged with nature's drives to shift you into overdrive.*

You are pocketed in your most relevant and advantageous place within nature's dynamic database and adaptation engine. You are integrated into the dynamic flow of synergistic living systems helping each other to adapt and advance for survival. You are positioned to receive the greatest support from surrounding biosystems for whatever goal you are pursuing that is in keeping with the maximization of your system and/or that of the species.

Savantflow automatically connects you to nature's creative engine, its production line, manufacturing plant, or factory for generating new solutions to adaptation and evolution challenges. You'll be grouped with the ideal information systems to fuel your creations. *Savanting* is about how to position yourself effectively to harness and exploit the biological infrastructure around you to achieve beyond your potential. It is the science behind superachieving.

Brilliant breakthroughs from the nonbrilliant

You have already been introduced to the fact that partnering internal and external biology will dramatically increase your experience of knowledge leaps such as breakthroughs, coincidences, epiphanies, and flashes of genius.

What could you create or achieve if you continually advanced your savant domain with decades of breakthroughs? What would your legacy be over a lifetime? Where would your career be? It is no wonder our four iconic founders achieved so much. What competitor could keep pace with their life of leaps?

It may surprise you to learn that the breakthroughs of the brilliant and those of the ordinary may be equal in brilliance. And those breakthroughs need not be limited to those born with well-developed creative biochemistry and aptitudes. Nature's self-organizing process groups all living systems for "survival synergy"

– living systems that will share the right information, resources, or support needed by another living system while getting the same in return.

If you'll allow yourself to be positioned by this ordering process, you'll be grouped with the right information fuel at the right time for breakthroughs. Even noncreatives and the nonbrilliant may apply basic logic to see how pieces of relevant information might be re-combined for breakthroughs and creations.

And because we are meant to operate this way, both the bioflow compliance and the re-combining happen automatically in savantflows. Average intelligence is usually sufficient for the implementation process between these brilliant breakthroughs to end up with results which far exceed your identified potential. Hence the title of this book.

This is the formula that generated the worldchanging achievements of Jobs, Gates, Zuckerberg, and Bezos. It is this formula that built Apple, Microsoft, Facebook, and Amazon, respectively, around the advance of the savant domains of their founders. Think of the plethora of coincidences and facilitating events which clustered around each founder as they launched their companies. It was almost as if nature was providing arrows to say "Go in this direction. I will help you."

Key Gates information coincidence

The serendipitous discovery of a Popular Electronics article in 1974 led Bill Gates and Paul Allen to the idea of personal computing and their first operating-system customer. "When Paul showed me that magazine, there was no such thing as a software industry," Gates recalls. "We had the insight that you could create one. And we did." Gates admits, "That was the most important idea that I ever had."[45]

Key Zuckerberg information coincidence

In Zuckerberg's senior year at Phillips Exeter Academy, the student directory with headshots – "The Photo Address Book" – was put online. It was affectionately referred to as "the facebook." This was a fortuitous coincidence. Mark's various experiments with social networks at Harvard led him to the refinements necessary for the winning formula for his version of the Facebook to emerge and continuously evolve.

Steve Jobs information coincidences

In 1968, a 13-year-old Steve Jobs audaciously called up Bill Hewlett, co-founder of Hewlett Packard, to get parts for his school project. Hewlett was so impressed with Jobs that he gave him an internship which eventually led to a job. This provided Steve with the industry education he would need to launch and grow Apple at such a young age. Apple was started with almost no money because of a series of coincidences and knowledge leaps which Jobs instinctively discovered how to exploit.

In another coincidence, Steve was shown the first working graphical user interface (GUI) at Xerox PARC in December of 1979. This concept simplified all future Apple products – all Apple computers, the iPod, the iPad, the iPhone – so they could be used by a much wider, non-technical audience. Apple introduced the Lisa computer with a GUI on January 19, 1983.

Before GUIs, computer commands had to be entered laboriously by text into a keyboard. There was no mouse. With software like Microsoft Windows, icons, menus, buttons, and windows can now convey commands such as to open, delete, and move files.

Steve Jobs had cultivated a lifetime of serial breakthroughs, epiphanies and flashes of genius. He was greedy for more. Accordingly, he put a great deal of effort into creating office environments that "promoted encounters and unplanned collaborations", including working with Norman Foster to design what he hoped would be the world's best office. He felt that, "If a building doesn't encourage [collaboration], you'll lose a lot of innovation and the magic that's sparked by serendipity."

So he designed Apple's building to make people get out of their offices and mingle in the central atrium with people they might not otherwise see. Now, expand Steve's design concept far beyond an office into the totality of your reality and you will better understand the savanting science behind superachieving.

You want to collide with people and events in your reality. Steve recognized the power of a breakthrough way of life. Bill Gates set up a culture at Microsoft to court the same kind of serendipitous collaboration.

Jeff Bezos information coincidences

One of the most important coincidences launching Jeff on his stellar path, was the new computer science degree being launched at Princeton the year he realized he did not have the aptitude and passion to be colonizing space from a Physics degree behind Stephen Hawking. Large computer networks are a pivotal catalyst of his worldbuilding.

After Bezos' accidental discovery of a 2300% annual growth rate of the internet, an additional series of coincidences compelled Jeff to decide what internet business to start in order to capitalize on this once-in-a-generation phenomenon. Coincidences directed him to formulate the ultimate winning model for the launch of Amazon within days.

He discovered that the major book wholesalers had already compiled electronic lists of their inventory. They simply needed to be listed together on a single internet location where the book-buying public could search the available stock and place orders directly.

Coincidentally, the American Booksellers' Convention was the next day so Bezos could quickly learn everything he needed to know about the book business. He could also establish, in one location, all the important connections that he would need for Amazon to launch.

Jeff speaks from experience when he says, "There'll always be serendipity involved in discovery." He attributes all the serendipitous and facilitating events around Amazon's origins and his success to "planets aligning." "I believe that all startup companies need a huge amount of luck."

In his biography at the Academy of Achievement website, Bezos is quoted as saying, "One of the things everybody should realize is that any time a start-up company turns into a substantial company over the years, there was a lot of luck involved."[46]

He was further quoted on the same website, "There are a lot of entrepreneurs. There are a lot of people who are very smart, very hardworking, very few ever have the planetary alignment that leads to a tiny little company growing into something substantial. So that requires not only a lot of planning, a lot of hard work, a big team of people who are all dedicated, but it also requires that not only the planets align, but that you get a few galaxies in there aligning, too. That's certainly what happened to us."[47]

We now know that it was Jeff's alignment with nature's bio-maximizing machinery that was speeding Amazon's creation with information leaps, breakthroughs, coincidences and facilitating events rather than the planets aligning.

Nature favored the direction in which Bezos was going to maximize his own system and that of the human race. Amazon was a creation which advanced Jeff's savant domain. The bioflow supported this mission for creatively expressing his essence. The bioflow brought the magic that facilitated Jeff's worldbuilding.

As Jeff discovered, there is a noticeable reduction in the amount of work that one has to do when one is thus extended by the bioflow. Coincidences, breakthroughs, and other leaps are how the biological guidance system facilitates one's penetration into unknown territory such as the launch of an Amazon. It groups you with the information and the connections you need when you need them. The guidance system ensures you are moving in the direction that is relevant to the evolution of humanity.

> *When we engage in what we are naturally suited to do, our work takes on the quality of play and it is play that stimulates creativity.* Linda Naiman

[42] Steven Kotler, *Flow States and Creativity: Can you train people to be more creative?* Psychology Today, Feb 25, 2014
https://www.psychologytoday.com/ca/blog/the-playing-field/201402/flow-states-and-creativity?amp
[43] *IBM 2010 Global CEO Study: Creativity Selected as Most Crucial Factor for Future Success*, News Release, Armonk, NY, May 18, 2010.
https://www-03.ibm.com/press/us/en/pressrelease/31670.wss
[44] Steven Kotler, *Flow States and Creativity: Can you train people to be more creative?* Psychology Today, Feb 25, 2014
[45] Drake Baer, *The Biggest Idea Bill Gates Ever Had,* October 11, 2013, *Fast Company*, https://www.fastcompany.com/3019834/the-biggest-idea-bill-gates-ever-had
[46] JR MacGregor, Jeff Bezos: The Force Behind the Brand: Insight and Analysis into the Life and Accomplishments of the Richest Man on the Planet, February 12, 2018, CAC Publishing LLC
[47] American Academy of Achievement Interview, May 4, 2001,
https://www.achievement.org/achiever/jeffrey-p-bezos/

15

Creativity from NonCreatives

Almost all creativity requires purposeful play.
Abraham Maslow

While "innovation" improves an existing system, "creativity" merges existing information systems to generate an entirely new unprecedented system. In Chapter 3, I noted that American cognitive psychologist Howard Gardner claimed that we are only creative in one or a few domains in which we have expertise. Therefore, before you label yourself uncreative, it's important to assume you are only creative in your savant domain.

In addition, researchers such as Harvard's Teresa Amabile have studies which show that creativity increases during flow states. Because of biological maximization, bioflow compliance, and activity fusion, savantflows will increase creativity even more.

Therefore, in your savant domain you might be tremendously creative, especially if the bioflow is feeding you the right information at the right time to fuel it. With savanting, even noncreatives may become creative. Simply choose savant-domain activities which will incite savantflows. This is the formula for your greatest creations.

Many assume Steve Jobs is synonymous with creativity and Bill Gates is not. Yet, both men changed the world. Let's explore these assumptions to see what we can learn about savanting's creativity and how to exploit it for your own worldchanging creations.

Bill's creativity questioned

Steve Jobs said of Gates, "Bill is basically unimaginative and has never invented anything, which is why I think he's more comfortable now in philanthropy than technology." "He just shamelessly ripped off other people's ideas."[48]

Yale University computer science professor, David Gelernter, wrote in "Time" magazine in 1998 that he believes Gates is overrated as a pioneer and entrepreneur. "Bill Gates is an American unoriginal." "It can be wiser to follow than to lead." Gelernter contends that Microsoft often makes products by re-combining ideas that already exist in the marketplace.

Isn't this the very definition of creativity in the savanting paradigm? Steve Jobs' own definition confirms it: "Creativity is just connecting things. When you ask creative people how they did something, they feel a little guilty because they didn't really do it, they just saw something. It seemed obvious to them after a while. That's because they were able to connect experiences they've had and synthesize new things."

Bill Gates' genius arises from his talent for re-combining entities throughout his life to generate the unprecedented – software programs, businesses, organizations, industries, governments, OED computer manufacturers, philanthropists, charitable organizations, and so on as he aged. His creativity can't be confined to Jobs' limited world of device invention.

In the infancy of Microsoft before Bill's consciousness had expanded, he could address the creation of a program or later, the re-combining of existing programs, to invent a new program which he would then modify and enhance.

However, with years of savantflows triggering the expansion of his consciousness, Gates' ability to re-combine what exists expanded to larger entities. Jobs savant domain and creativity was more like that of savants – narrow but deep. Comparing the creativity of the two men is like comparing an "Apple" to an orange.

Someone laid down the early structures of the personal computing and software industries – the licensing, structure, standards, and rules of operation behind it. Creativity occurred. Can anyone really suggest Bill Gates was not the key creator? Especially as he does the same for the field of philanthropy and through it to many aspects of the infrastructure underpinning our society.

There can be little doubt about Bill's talent for generating the foundations for new frontiers, governments, organizations, industries, and markets. Microsoft thrived locked into the marketplace by Bill's brilliant business constructs, innovations, and partnerships which made its less-than-stellar technology number one.

Because Jobs did not recognize Bill's creativity beyond technology, he did not cultivate it in himself. This was undoubtedly a contributing factor to his being fired from Apple for a decade and the creation of a culture which took Apple to the brink of bankruptcy. The brilliance of Job's design required him to relentlessly commit to a narrow focus. This dedicated focus is a key contributor to the brilliance of his designs.

Is Jobs' creativity different?
The executive summary
Let me overview my response to this question before going into detail with examples. Both entrepreneurs had the same intent – to

better the lives of individuals *en masse*. Both were merged within the bioflow evolving the human race, so they generated products at the forefront of humanity's evolution. Both were being fed the right information at the right time by the bioflow to catalyze creativity in their respective savant domains.

Their missions overlapped for most of their careers in the field of personal computing, which – as we have already seen with their success outside of that field – did not define either of their savant domains. The creativity of Jobs and Gates are, by definition, the same. Both re-combined existing systems to create an unprecedented system.

However, how they arrived at their end results was different. Jobs used more creative inspiration where the creative re-combination occurred in his head. It was achieved by breakthroughs fueled by information systems from the bioflow. His quote earlier in the chapter reinforces an internal remix.

Gates, on the other hand, used more logic with the re-combining information occurring externally. It was fueled by coincidences, models and facilitating people and events generated by the bioflow. His creativity was more action-based.

Their savant domains are different. Bill's is broad and big picture. Steve's was narrow, deep and detailed. Bill's consciousness or span of purview was significantly wider. This increased his source of fuel for his creations and the information systems he re-combined were bigger.

Gates built the Microsoft product line and business through partnering and inclusion for shared prosperity. Jobs' strategy was more isolating by design. He structured Apple initially to have an exclusive, proprietary, and independent product line which did not mesh well with others.

However, he seemed to model Gates' inclusion approach when he returned to Apple to rescue it from bankruptcy after his ten-year absence. Pixar's work with Disney and others may also have contributed to his transformation as well.

Jobs came to allow others to generate applications for his exclusive product line which helped him to defeat competition such as Blackberry which followed Jobs into exclusion but missed his redirection to inclusion. Blackberry missed the app bandwagon that saved Apple – especially with its iPhone market penetration. Without a plethora of device-compliant applications, functionality and personalization were greatly reduced.

The GUIs incident

Let me reveal some of the historical events upon which I based these opinions. While at Apple, Steve Jobs contracted Bill Gates at Microsoft to write new software to provide the graphical user interfaces (GUIs) that were so critical to so many of Jobs' greatest inventions.

These interfaces would allow a user to interact with electronic devices through graphical icons and visual indicators rather than having to type commands on a keyboard. As you might imagine, requiring users to learn a plethora of keyboard commands would present an intimidating barrier to entry for most.

Bill Gates was enthralled with the idea of graphical user interfaces and wanted to use them for Microsoft instead of Apple. Unfortunately, it would be unethical to steal a client's idea. Fortunately, Bill *coincidentally* discovered that Jobs had learned the idea from products both Apple and Microsoft people had seen at Xerox PARC. Xerox had revealed what they had developed in the hopes that known producers such as Apple and Microsoft would buy the technology or help Xerox to commercialize it.

Therefore, GUIs were not Steve Jobs' proprietary idea. It would therefore be fair game for Bill to develop software with graphical user interfaces for Microsoft instead. This led to the birth of Windows, a system that uses a mouse to drive a graphic interface which displayed text and images on the screen. Windows was quite an improvement over the text-and-keyboard-driven MS-DOS operating system.

Needless to say, when Jobs heard about Windows, he went ballistic. This led to Apple initiating a court case which was later dismissed as being without merit. But fair is fair. This is how creativity works – new creations emerge by re-combining existing information systems.

While Bill may have sourced software from the marketplace, he was quite clever about adapting and enhancing it for greater market receptivity. He did the same with Xerox's GUIs.

He did not directly copy what Xerox had done. Rather, Gates combined Xerox's ideas with the trends in his reality and other information systems plus his years of programming finesse to achieve a significantly more advanced outcome with Windows. Bill was just as creative but didn't see the need to start from scratch as Jobs did.

Might I also note in Gates' defense that, despite his criticism of Bill for "ripping off the ideas of others," Jobs was unconsciously doing exactly the same thing with what he had learned from Xerox. This is not a criticism. This is simply the way creativity works for evolution's adaptivity, for the uber-creative Steve Jobs, and for all of us ordinary folk.

Creative tension

Had Jobs realized this basic underlying dynamic of creativity on an implementation level, he might not have suffered the stresses and strains of the creative tension arising from demanding so much originality from himself and others. I think this creative tension led to issues with his temper, his toxic disparagement of others, and the health problems that plagued him. Even a dedication to mindfulness meditation could not dissipate all the creative tension he experienced.

It was undoubtedly this disposition and temperament which caused Jobs to launch a smear campaign against Gates. As we have seen, Jobs respected Gates enough to hire Microsoft for software development. According to his authorized biography, Jobs kept a note from Bill Gates beside his deathbed.[49] All was not what it seemed between them. It would appear that many have had a plethora of wrong impressions about Bill Gates for decades.

Different savant domains

What Jobs and others assumed was Bill Gates' savant domain was, in fact, not. As a reminder, "domain" and "field" or "industry" are not interchangeable in savanting. Existing epithets, fields, and categories may not apply.

Your savant domain is based on the maximization of your biological wiring. The bioflow maximizing machinery decides what your savant domain is at any moment in time based on the theme of which intrinsically or biologically rewarding activities incite your savantflows.

Jeff Bezos knew the truth about Gates when he switched disciplines from physics and Stephen Hawking's space to computer science and Bill Gates' worldbuilding. Yes, it is Bezos and Gates who are comparable not Jobs.

Jobs is the artist who strived for perfection in design to produce devices that were universally loved aesthetically and functionally. Steve was an aesthetic idealist to whom it was more important to create the best product than to sell the most. He had passion and vision for what technology could do in people's lives and the magnetic charisma and incredible showmanship to promote his devices. Steve Jobs is truly a legend in the field of innovative and interactive design.

For Jobs, software was merely the means to run his devices, make them more endearing and better able to enhance the lives of consumers. For Gates and Bezos, it was the means to advance the structural underpinnings of civilization globally. For Zuckerberg, it was the means to unite humanity by creating, reinforcing, and joining the constellation of relationships of each individual. For all four, it was about bettering the quality of life of individuals en masse.

Bill Gates has a proven history of a logic-sourced creativity that even noncreatives might emulate. Gates took existing technology, adapted it to a specific market, and then dominated that market through innovative promotion and shrewd business savvy.

For example, Gates shrewdly chose not to offer to transfer to IBM the copyright on the MS-DOS operating system Microsoft was hired by IBM to write because he believed that other hardware vendors would clone IBM's system. This was Gates' form of brilliant creativity. And he was right.

Much as he had anticipated, after the first IBM PCs were released, cloners such as Compaq began producing compatible PCs, and the market was soon flooded with clones. Rather than produce their own operating systems, the cloners decided it was cheaper to purchase MS-DOS off the shelf.

As a result, MS-DOS became the standard operating system for the industry. By 1993, Windows was selling at a rate of 1 million copies per month and was estimated to be running on nearly 85 percent of the world's computers. Microsoft's sales soared from $7 million in 1980 to $16 million in 1981.

A single creative business move may have generated the bulk of Microsoft's revenue. Jobs, David Gelernter, and others had missed the true creativity and worldchanging breakthroughs of Bill Gates.

Microsoft solidified its industry dominance through another creative business move in the mid-1990s. They combined Windows with their other applications to create "suites," then persuaded leading computer makers to preload their software on every computer they sold. The strategy worked so well that by 1999 Microsoft was posting sales of $19.7 billion, and Gates' personal wealth had grown to a phenomenal $90 billion.

Gates' passion for global business changed how business was done both within his industries and other industries as well. He set standards, first with MS-DOS and later with Windows. These standards shaped the modern computer industry and will continue to influence its growth for decades.

And now, he is repeating the process to generate new standards, structure, and strategy for more impactful mega-philanthropy to ensure it will cause permanent transformation in the world. The message here is that the real magic of the science behind savanting occurs in one's savant domain. For those craving global impact, honor internal and external biology. Exploit biology to live a life of serial creativity and breakthroughs that will evolve humanity.

Vision from nonvisionaries

Bill Gates was criticized in the 1990s for not recognizing the power and potential of the internet. He was accused of not being visionary. Gates admits he did not embrace the Web until 1996, two years after browsers debuted. However, this does not mean this was the wrong decision for him or Microsoft.

It is not necessary to "see" trends if one is using the signals to move moment by moment with the bioflow evolutionary engine that is generating those trends. The bioflow would have been orchestrating the maximum of Gates' system within the maximization of the Microsoft system within the maximization process for humanity's system.

There is lots of evidence that Gates' was attuned to the evolutionary advance of those three systems as well as those within his savant domain. Just by continuing to do intrinsically rewarding work every day, he could experience all the benefits of knowing trends without knowing them.

What appeared in 20/20 hindsight to be smart business strategy may in fact be simply compliance with the bioflow day after day as he had done since childhood because he had never lost the connection into which each of us are born.

Nonvisionaries can thus proceed as if they are insightful visionaries. By moving with the trendsetting bioflow engine one may exploit the trends to maximize within one's savant domain. This is another way that the ordinary may achieve the extraordinary.

With 20/20 hindsight, the signals did not fail Gates. Microsoft's browser, Internet Explorer, benefited from having a few years to see what features of other browsers were most valued. Microsoft could then capitalize on the best of the browsers to *leapfrog* them to create a product ahead of them all.

In yet another seemingly brilliant business breakthrough, Gates was then able to prevail in the browser market by bundling Internet Explorer with the Windows operating system, Internet Service Provider software, and new PCs from OEMs.

Thus, without the requirement for a user-initiated installation, Microsoft could lock consumers into its browser solution before users even had a chance to acquire and try another browser. Gates had not only caught up to the Netscape browser lead but *leapfrogged* ahead as he did with the Xerox GUIs.

The Netscape browser ultimately died despite its rapid success after early market entry. This was yet another business decision made by Bill Gates that locked in Microsoft revenues. It was not the browser "technology" which made the money. It was Gates' savvy and creativity in inventing new business infrastructure in the frontiers of his savant domain.

Not everyone needs to have the creative mind of a Jobs or the venturing prowess of a Bezos to have creative breakthroughs. *Noncreatives and nonvisionaries may proceed in partnership with the bioflow as if they have both creativity and vision.* You are about to learn some of the ways in which the four iconic founders exploited the dynamic flow of information all around them as byproducts of this incredible biological guidance system.

As Bill Gates proves, despite his not having the technology visionary capabilities of a Steve Jobs, he was still able to sustain his position at the forefront of technology trends. He moved Microsoft at top speed to greater success than Apple by not just assimilating existing technologies but using them as *springboards* to jump ahead.

More about *leapfrogging* and *springboarding* in Chapter 17 to capitalize on environmental scanning to increase your creativity and creations. Technology vision is only a small part of Bill Gates' savant domain for bettering the lives of people. His vision and creativity in the invention of the business infrastructure portion of his savant domain are unsurpassed.

Bill's partnership with nature's bio-underpinnings was working perfectly. Again, with 20/20 hindsight, Gates' decision to focus on Windows in the mid-nineties over the internet was the right one for him and for Microsoft, even if the nay-sayers were correct and he seemingly did not have the vision to realize its value.

He analyzed the signposts inside and outside of himself correctly and took the right action as if he was a visionary. Significant revenues from the internet did not really emerge until around 2004 as Gates, the supposed nonvisionary, had predicted 10 years earlier. Therefore, little was lost by delaying attention to a browser and much was in fact gained by focusing on Windows.

So far, we have explored how savanting facilitates "brilliant breakthroughs from the nonbrilliant," "creativity from noncreatives" and "vision from nonvisionaries." Now we want to investigate how savanting enables "exceptional execution from the execution-challenged."

---

[48] Walter Isaacson, *Steve Jobs*, October 24, 2011, Simon & Schuster
[49] Walter Isaacson, *Steve Jobs*, October 24, 2011, Simon & Schuster

16

Creative Concept vs Creative Execution

To me, ideas are worth nothing unless executed.
They are just a multiplier.
Execution is worth millions. Steve Jobs

It's not about ideas.
It's about making ideas happen.
Scott Belsky, Co-Founder, Behance

The thing that keeps a business ahead of the
competition is excellence in execution.
Tom Peters

Having a vision for what you want is not enough.
Vision without execution is hallucination.
Thomas A. Edison

Ideation without execution is delusion.
Robin Sharma

A really great talent finds its happiness in execution.
Johann Wolfgang von Goethe

Success doesn't necessarily come from breakthrough
innovation but from flawless execution. A great
strategy alone won't win a game or a battle; the win
comes from basic blocking and tackling.
Naveen Jain

In the Wall Street Journal in December 2012, economist, Robert J. Gordon, noted that the slowdown in innovation is due to the end of big breakthroughs.[50] Nobel Laureate in economics, Edmund S. Phelps disagreed. He responded to Gordon's position in the "Opinionator" at the "New York Times" in February 2013. He said that "innovation has declined in the everyday processes that businesses tinker with incrementally as they try to become more productive over time."[51]

The argument for us, then, is, "Does superachieving come from having "the big idea" or from generating the thousands of breakthroughs and creative solutions that emerge from the work of execution experts implementing that idea?"

I am with Phelps. In today's fast-paced world of the instantaneous spread of ideas, rapid-fire creative adaptation and execution are the name of the game.

One idea vs thousands?

Many aspiring entrepreneurs believe that they must come up with a big idea in order to become superachievers. Yet it's not those with the big idea who have become our worldchangers in recent years. Rather, *it is those with the thousands of innovative implementation ideas that are superachieving and being valued by the world the most.*

It is *the execution creatives* who are so critical to the advance of our civilization. In this century, intuitive implementers will be more important than the idea-makers and the inventors.

Steve Jobs clearly chose execution over ideas: "You know, one of the things that really hurt Apple was after I left John Sculley got a very serious disease. It's the disease of thinking that a really great idea is 90 percent of the work. And if you just tell all these other people 'here's this great idea,' then of course they can go off and make it happen. And the problem with that is that there's just a tremendous amount of craftsmanship in between a great idea and a great product."[52]

Steve Wozniak's brilliant Macintosh technology would never have reached the heights of Apple if it were not for the packaging and creative execution by Steve Jobs.

The same is true of Mike Lazaridis' invention of the breakthrough technology of BlackBerry. It took the brilliance of expansionist, dealmaker, and execution driver, Jim Balsillie – Mike's co-CEO – to take BlackBerry global.

The idea of Facebook was certainly not that original in an environment littered with social networks. However, it was the best executed idea. It was rolled out with endless adaptation, innovation, and responsiveness to member demands for privacy, security and more. It was continuously shaped by Zuckerberg's innate genius and passion for bonding communities.

Mark's focus on expansion, for example, despite no revenues, paid off when advertisers flocked to Facebook to capitalize on the massive number of members.

In the hit 2010 movie, "The Social Network," about the founding of Facebook Zuckerberg says of the Winklevosses, "If you guys were the inventors of Facebook, you'd have invented Facebook."

The Zuckerberg character brings home the point about execution finesse by saying, "You have part of my attention – you have the minimum amount. The rest of my attention is back at the offices of Facebook, where my colleagues and I are doing things that no one in this room, including and especially your clients, are intellectually or creatively capable of doing."

"The Winklevoss twins expected that their one social network idea – that was neither implemented for Facebook nor original – entitled them to earn the profits that were generated by the thousands of events of innovation, adaptation, and execution creativity that Zuckerberg, his friends, and his team had to do daily to create and advance Facebook to the success that it is today.

Amazon was not the first e-commerce website; it was simply the best executed every day from the launch. While Bezos' programming genius might have launched Amazon, it is his captivation with incessant invention and history-making venturing into new territory – his true paid play – that has sustained Amazon's global prominence.

Spirited creativity and adaptivity differentiated the unparalleled execution expertise of Jeff Bezos from the exhaustive number of me-too e-commerce retailers on the internet. Through *ongoing breakthrough-by-breakthrough execution*, Jeff could keep Amazon ahead of even those who would try to copy his execution ideas.

One-click shopping, customer reviews, and e-mail order verification were all unprecedented before Jeff. In 2011, Jeff and Amazon Lab126 president, Gregg Zehr, won "The Economist's" annual "Innovation Award" for their work on the Kindle e-book reader making it an original equipment manufacturer (OEM). This handheld electronic reading device promotes ease of reading. Later versions rivalled the Apple iPad.

Jeff's penchant from childhood for endlessly initiating a "garageful" of experiments is key to the company's success. In Jeff's words, "If you double the number of experiments you do per year, you're going to double your inventiveness."

At Jeff's hand, serial business model upgrades became routine at Amazon. One new value proposition offered a commission-based brokerage service to buyers and sellers of used books. Another business-model change provided third-party sellers with a sales-and-service model that paid Amazon commissions on the sales of its competitors.

Yet another new business model launched a web services platform for IT customers. A seamlessly integrated iTunes-type digital media platform was created to support the product. This business model was potentially disruptive to the entire publishing industry. Within five years the site used by Amazon's web-services platform had grown into the seventh largest in the world.

Microsoft's Windows may not have been the best software, but it was the best executed from a business perspective. In fact, Gates' business strategies surrounding Windows accounted for more revenue than having the best software ever could. Gates ultimately created a monopoly around using Windows in the PC world.

As brilliant as the Xerox PARC GUIs and other inventions were, the company could not execute. That is why they were courting proven producers such as Apple and Microsoft.

The Execution Creatives

The founders of Microsoft, Apple, Facebook, and Amazon are innovative execution gurus. They are what I call *execution creatives*. Their success is not due to the idea that launched their companies. It was and is due to their continuously creative execution – their *serial execution creativity* at each decisionpoint of opportunistic implementation.

The term "opportunistic" is used to denote not only the opportunity to accelerate their planned project direction but perhaps from each advancing vantage point to see a bigger goal in the same direction or in a completely different direction.

One coincidence for example can eliminate hundreds of steps to rewrite not only the direction of the project but even its goal. Advancing by serial quantum leaps is a completely different paradigm of project management modus operandi than is the norm. Remember our six superachievers have been operating in partnership with the bioflow since childhood.

They live *bioflow-compliant*. They are merged with the bioflow guidance system which ensures that they are generating products and services at the forefront of humanity's evolution. Accordingly, the same bioflow information inflow which fuels ideas and creations also occurs during savantflows to fuel breakthroughs and epiphanies to enhance execution.

The coincidences, facilitating events, and epiphanies are all related to the forefront due to the maximization of each person-system within the maximization of their company system within the maximization of their industry system within the maximization of humanity's system. The four founders are operating in biological compliance internally and externally.

Accelerated execution from the execution-challenged

So, what do you do if you don't have the talents, aptitudes, and wherewithal to follow in the implementation footsteps of our four famous founders to make your dreams come true? You'll be happy to learn that the savanting protocol positions you not only for that first big idea but also for the multitude of ideas and breakthroughs it will take to implement that idea to its fullest.

Therefore, even the execution-challenged may "finesse" with the best of them in the same way that noncreatives can create with savanting. The principle is the same. Exploit and re-combine the clustering of relevant information systems that emerges from complying with the bioflow that is supporting your savantflows.

1. Merge your goals with bioflow goals

The most successful ideas for bioflow-supported execution are those which improve the operation of the system of humanity. In other words, the ones which further the goals of the bioflow yet require intrinsically rewarding activities that shift you into savantflow.

Then you can be sure you'll receive lots of support from the bioflow. Attaching to the bioflow guidance system as it adapts and evolves the human race provides both the direction of execution and the information fuel for serial breakthroughs to accelerate it. *All four companies of our famous founders are built on bioflow goals.*

2. Choose previously supported goals

Past bioflow support predicts future bioflow support. Therefore, choose the types of goals and projects which have been supported by the bioflow in your past to receive execution support in the future. You may not have goals or don't know where you want to go. However, you can get started at top speed by igniting your biology. Use intrinsically rewarding activities to stimulate savantflows. Do as many as you can during a short time span. The pattern and direction will emerge.

3. Exploit the bioflow guidance system and resources

Treat your reality like a giant computer with a GPS guidance system and you'll have what you need for both the big idea and the creative execution needed to capture its potential. Move in sync with the signals you've learned indicating when you are attached to the bioflow evolutionary engine advancing humanity.

If you're going where civilization is going, your products are going to be well received. Your life will be filled with leaps and facilitating events. You'll have directions for penetrating unknown territory at the forefront of civilization's history with new safety and surefootedness.

In addition to complying with the bioflow's maximizing drives, you'll also want to follow nature's drives for self-organizing. If you will allow yourself to be orchestrated by nature's self-organizing process, you'll find yourself colliding with the right information at the right time for the transformations, breakthroughs, coincidences, implementation models, and facilitating people and events that you'll need next for exceptional execution. The bioflow's got you covered.

4. Exploit savant-domain drives

Even if you can't execute well in any other territory, it is possible for you to superexecute in your own savant domain. You'll be pulled ahead by your passion, your drives, your emotional highs, and your addiction to savantflows.

You've already learned how to identify your savant domain and thus the territory of bioflow support from an examination of the event patterns in your past – your themes of unpaid work, creativity-pursuit, savantflows, frontier-pursuit, spontaneous knowledge, knowledge-pursuit theme, meaning-pursuit, growth-pursuit, intrinsically rewarding activities, work-that-is-play, and so on. In no time, great execution will be irresistible. Even the execution-challenged may execute brilliantly when they honor their savant formula.

5. Use environmental scanning at each decision point

You will want to take the time to survey the events in your reality relevant to your project as you take each decision on how to advance. If you discover information fuel, you'll want to see if you can re-combine it to leap ahead on the execution. In the next chapter you'll learn how to use *leapfrogging* and *springboarding* to increase opportunistic execution.

6. Grow yourself to grow your creations

If you grow yourself, you will grow your realities. It will be easier to implement realities that are bigger than you normally experience. Be aware of your information structure. No matter what your intent, it is this upon which the bioflow is acting. If you are not being grouped with relevant systems, change your beliefs and emotional signature to change to a more advantageous information infrastructure. This will ensure you are connected with systems more facilitating to your project execution.

7. Recruit execution geniuses

This point is discussed below in the next two sections.

Execution geniuses, prodigies and junkies

There are those whose savant domain is execution creativity and nothing else. This is what they crave to do. This is their work-that-is-play. They can implement in any field better than the experts in that field. Execution talent is pure serial creativity. It is opportunistic and organic.

Execution creatives intuitively partner with the bioflow to court coincidences and to fuel breakthroughs to catapult the project ahead. They have likely demonstrated their talent right from childhood – perhaps even being child prodigies or execution savants in a territory where this capability is seldom tracked.

But, more than a talent for implementation, these execution creatives have a passion for it – a benevolent addiction to it. They are achievement junkies.

Somehow, magically, when they scan reality, they see the gates and pathways that are open for accelerating projects that no one else can see – especially as their consciousness expands with serial savantflows. By using bioflow support for execution, they can achieve the same speed of implementation whether they are moving into known or unknown territory. The procedure is the same at each decisionpoint.

I think we've seen particular evidence of execution genius in Jeff Bezos, Bill Gates, and Mark Zuckerberg in particular. Since their domains are so well developed, I believe execution creativity is a secondary skill they've picked up by partnering with the bioflow as their usual modus operandi for decades. You can do the same.

Partnering with Execution Creatives

It takes some time to learn to maneuver with the bioflow to advantage for execution. You may therefore wish to bridge that gap by partnering with a natural execution creative even if s/he know nothing about your field.

As one's partnership with the bioflow solidifies, everyone can become an execution creative. However, until you have mastered your own execution creativity using savanting, entice someone whose savant domain is execution creativity to work on your projects to not only accelerate your progress but to teach you how they do what they do.

This is what Mike Lazaridis did for BlackBerry. He was an execution creative for technology development but not for its spread globally. He needed Jim Balsillie for that. The same was true of Wozniak with respect to Jobs. Those who have donated massive amounts to Bill Gates' mega-philanthropy are relying on the incredible execution creativity of this worldbuilder to put it to the best use.

The pull to advance one's savant domain

Despite the opinion of the Winklevoss twins or how events were misrepresented in "The Social Network" movie, it is essential for prospective superachievers to realize that, if the Winklevoss twins had never existed, Zuckerberg would still have developed the next advance in global bonding and the next, and next, and so on.

Facebook is an expression of Mark's savant domain. Facebook did not and does not define his savant domain. If Facebook disappeared, Mark would still advance global community-building. It is not the success of the idea that is resulting in Mark's success. *It is his biological predisposition to advance his savant domain.*

This is what drives the thousands of innovations, creations, and flashes of genius that have made Facebook successful. Therefore, in addition to exploiting nature's guidance system, this is another aspect driving excellent execution.

It is not the idea. It is the pull and the passion to execute within one's savant domain that results in the success of our four iconic founders and other superachievers. It is the innate pull to work-that-is-play for them. This is the true formula behind their success. This is the ideal career strategy that you will want to emulate whether in your own company, a job, or working on a project to develop your next creation.

QUOTES FROM MICHAEL DELL, founder and CEO of Dell Technologies, one of the world's largest technology infrastructure companies. He was ranked as the 39th richest person in the world by Forbes with a net worth of $28.6 billion as of September 2018:

- *Ideas are a commodity. Execution of them is not.*
- *By questioning all the aspects of our business, we continuously inject improvement and innovation into our culture.*
- *Whether you've found your calling, or if you're still searching, passion should be the fire that drives your life's work.*

[50]   Robert J. Gordon, Why Innovation Won't Save Us. For more than a century, the U.S. economy grew robustly thanks to big inventions; those days are gone, December 21, 2012, The Wall Street Journal, https://www.wsj.com/articles/SB10001424127887324461604578191781756437940

[51]   Edmund S. Phelps, Less Innovation, More Inequality, February 2013, the Opinionator, the New York Times, https://opinionator.blogs.nytimes.com/author/edmund-s-phelps/

[52]   *Robert X. Cringley,* Steve Jobs - The Lost Interview, *1996,* PBS special, *"Triumph of the Nerds"* https://www.youtube.com/watch?v=TRZAJY23xio

17

Environmental Scanning to fuel Breakthroughs

As you advance your savant domain with serial savantflows, you'll come to routinely survey your reality for relevant information to be re-combined to solve problems and accelerate execution. You'll come to realize there is a dynamic order all around you despite your lifetime assumption of disorder and chaos in your reality.

Everything changes when you are maximized – when you are extended by nature's bio-infrastructure. Look for that order in your savant domain and capitalize on it to become self-actualized.

Exploit the information fuel in your reality

We want to demonstrate, using the lives of our four founding superachievers, how to become more opportunistic in capitalizing on the flow of systems around you. You'll want to start to pay attention to the events and information pieces that emerge in your reality. To the uneducated eye, reality appears chaotic. Its dynamic order is not evident to the uninformed.

However, you now know that living information systems like human beings are grouped by nature's self-organizing process for "survival synergy." Systems that can help each other are grouped together. Savanting exploits this order within the seeming chaos.

If you are moving towards your maximum, the external bio-machinery will engage and orchestrate you to the right information at the right time for spontaneous knowledge, sudden creations, coincidences, and other serendipitous leaps that will catapult you to your goals.

Springboarding

A springboard is a point of departure or a jumping-off point. Zuckerberg's first meeting with the Winklevoss twins was a springboard to a different direction of thinking. Knowing what he did not like about their idea clarified the direction Mark preferred to go. It was never a matter of copying their idea. They were interested in copying Match.com but limiting it to Harvard students. The twins wanted to meet girls.

Zuckerberg was interested in expanding and improving on a Friendster.com model. Harvard would just be the start in his expansion plan. As a brilliant execution creative, what Zuckerberg saw was a rollout strategy school by school globally until it could be opened to the public. He marked his progress in terms of number of members.

The twins were unintentionally a springboard for strategies that the twins had never even considered. But the twins were only one of many events in Zuckerberg's reality which could have and would have triggered Mark's "springboarding."

As we have seen, Zuckerberg had been working on social networks since he was a child. He already had lots of relevant Facebook pieces in his life. Meeting the twins merely triggered his thinking on how to combine them going forward to better achieve his goal and the emotional state of being he was seeking.

Oftentimes, the addition of a single piece of information may trigger the transaction which capitalizes on everything pertinent you have accumulated to date. A single event may catalyze seemingly disparate pieces into a meaningful breakthrough or solution. Zuckerberg's rethinking on meeting with the twins may have been the one missing piece to make something of all the pieces that he had collected already in his savant domain.

If the twins had not been the source of the information fuel that Zuckerberg needed next to catalyze his creative process, any of a thousand other sources would have taken their place. When you partner with internal and external biology maximizing mechanisms, nature's librarian will group you with synergistic information systems to fuel the advantageous re-combinings. That is what will generate your breakthroughs and unprecedented creations.

This community-building was Mark's life theme from childhood. Zuckerberg is biologically wired for emotional highs and peak performance when pursuing this theme.

In the words of Jeff Bezos, "You want to look at what other companies are doing. It's very important not to be hermetically sealed. But you don't want to look at it as if, 'OK, we're going to copy that.' You want to look at it and say, 'That's very interesting. What can we be inspired to do as a result of that?' And then put your own unique twist on it."

Springboarding would accurately describe what happened when Jobs and Gates learned of Xerox PARC's unprecedented graphical user interfaces (GUIs). Suddenly planned ideas for Microsoft's Windows and Apple's hardware and software products were instantly rewritten. Each did not copy Xerox's products but "springboarded" into the directions that worked from re-combining existing information systems in their respective environments.

Leapfrogging

A springboard event catalyzes past information pieces into a new information system – whether there is a breakthrough in understanding or a new physical creation. In contrast, you will come to use *leapfrogging* to skip the implementation of the next few physical iterations to speed your progress. Leapfrog is a game in which one player vaults over another.

Netscape was *leapfrogged* by Microsoft's Internet Explorer jumping ahead of where Netscape was going rather than where Netscape's current iteration was. Apple and Microsoft products continuously *leapfrogged* beyond each other in a way that benefited all of us. You may *leapfrog* beyond even "unexecuted ideas" not just the physical implementations in your reality to secure your lead.

Assume everything is grouped beneficially in your savant domain – for *springboarding*, for *leapfrogging*, for re-combining for breakthroughs, or to stop you from going in this direction, or to entice you to proceed into another direction.

Sometimes you don't know an event's use until more information is grouped in your reality. Then the re-combining bursts forth in a major Aha! event. Therefore, you will want to store unused savant-domain events in your mind until the reason for their existence becomes evident. "Peak Evolution" provides more details on how to partner with reality to speed achievement for those who wish it.

Your savant-domain "book"

You will want to source as much information relevant to your next savant-domain frontier as possible. The more information you have, the more likely it is that you will find the best possible "re-combinings" for breakthroughs and sudden leaps. One way to increase your information is to access the "book" for your entire domain. This is your goal.

You may recall that access to "books" or systems of information occurs in your savant domain as with savants. Remember Jim Carrey's access to comedian Andy Kaufman's "personbook" as he played him in the biopic "Man on the Moon?" I believe all four founders experienced this ability as they did their "work-that-is-play" in savant-domain flow states.

However, as with savants, the access goes beyond what has been physically absorbed through one's five senses. Imagine each of these four superachievers as if they were a spider sitting on a web that is their savant domain.

The slightest movement anywhere throughout the web would catch their eye. It is almost as if they would sense a frequency change with any new information entering their savant domain. This ability would increase over time as their consciousnesses expanded with savantflows.

Protect yourself from simultaneous, inevitable creations – The BlackBerry Plight

I had mentioned earlier that this access to the "books" of one's domain was an explanation for scientists who discover or develop the same things simultaneously in different parts of the world without awareness of each other.

It is important for you to embrace the totality of your domain. If those in your savant domain are routinely accessing the same "book" as you for your whole domain, then they will have access to all the same pieces as you do to re-combine to generate new creations or breakthroughs.

The chances of duplications then will be high. As a result, there will be simultaneous inevitable creations in various parts of the globe. You will want to capitalize on this situation. However, you will also want to protect you and your creations from it. All four of our founders faced repercussions from simultaneous creations.

Many of the inventions that we have thought were profound were inevitable given the big picture of trends. They were part of a very observable progression. When your consciousness expands from years in savantflows as with our four, you'll see the patterns, trends, and themes more easily to be able to exploit them to advance your savant domain. You'll see all the pieces and how they may be re-combined for industry or humanity breakthroughs.

You will more routinely follow the path of Bill Gates, for example, in adding the additional inventions and discoveries of others to your breakthroughs going forward. You'll assume others are moving in the same direction and just sense when there are new inventions or breakthroughs on the horizon that can be used to advance your own work.

An example of the need to protect yourself from simultaneous and inevitable creations in your savant domain is illustrated by the BlackBerry story. Given the progression of the internet and wireless technology, BlackBerry's "wireless email" was as inevitable as a Facebook in the field of social networking. The same is true of graphical user interfaces (GUIs) from Apple and Microsoft in the field of personal computers with the dedication of both to being user-friendly.

The BlackBerry is a much-loved line of wireless handheld devices and services designed and marketed by BlackBerry Limited which was previously called Research in Motion (RIM). BlackBerry products have evolved from a wireless email pager in 1999 through smartphones starting in 2003 and continuing today.

The BlackBerry was so revolutionary and addictive when it first came out that it earned the affectionate nickname of "crackberry."

BlackBerry wireless email devices were first invented by two Canadian engineering students, Mike Lazaridis and Douglas Fregin. As with our four founders, they had the first, best execution of an idea that was trending. I'm certain that is why McLean-based NTP Inc. sued RIM for allegedly copying wireless mail-delivery technology it had invented. A U.S. jury found Canada's BlackBerry guilty of patent infringement back in 2002.

There were a lot of red flags clouding this decision – not the least of which was whether a patent should ever have been issued to NTP Inc. in the first place given inevitable industry trends. Inventions cannot be patented if they would be obvious "to a person having ordinary skill in the art to which the claimed invention pertains."

NTP's patent did not meet the requirement for "non-obvious" improvement over prior art, especially now that you know about the capabilities and spontaneous knowledge of people such as our four icons operating in their savant domain. Yet RIM had to pay a post-court settlement of $612.5 million, far exceeding Zuckerberg's pre-court settlement to the Winklevoss twins of $65 million.

My verdict would always go to the one who owns the savant domain in which the invention occurred. The work of inventor Mike Lazaridis and Douglas Fregin before and after their invention of the BlackBerry proves that *their inventions were "inevitable developments"* in their *"savant domain."*

Their invention was a natural extension of their other inventions in a field littered with similar inventions as a result of everyone re-combining the same precursors. The same pieces of the end product were merged, built upon, and adapted by others in different ways in many parts of the globe.

If the Winklevoss twins had invented Facebook, and the inventors at NTP had invented the Blackberry, they both would have had many more such developments in the same fields. That this was their savant domain would be obvious.

This, of course, is not the case. Both Lazaridis/Fregin and Zuckerberg were addicted to and obsessed by their savant domains. Their success was not due to accidental discoveries or theft of the work of others. They were both immersed in the evolutionary processes advancing their savant domain.

As with Zuckerberg, Lazaridis was penalized for having *the best execution* which was due in part to his co-founder and co-CEO of Research in Motion, Jim Balsillie. As an imperialistic dealmaker, Jim too was immersed in his own savant domain with his own perpetual flashes of genius. His business, deal-making, and leadership inventions equaled the engineering inventions of his co-CEO, Mike Lazaridis.

Balsillie could not resist making deal after deal to bring the BlackBerry to country after country as well as to every business and consumer frontier associated with its advance. Jim's endless creativity and drive for execution accounted for the BlackBerry's phenomenal market share until 2010 and his operational departure.

There was a talented expansionist team behind Jim under BlackBerry COO, Don Morrison, which was responsible for what may arguably be one of the fastest global expansions to date. Within 10 years this team increased BlackBerry revenues from $70 million to more than $20 billion. Operations expanded from 2 countries to 175. This required negotiating partnerships with more than 550 carriers and creating products in almost 30 languages.

Why should the questionable patent of McLean-based NTP Inc. be paid for by the superior execution of Balsillie's team? The precursors for what Lazaridis developed were available to many.

Simultaneous and inevitable invention of wireless email devices was a given.

Why could the BlackBerry not be developed simultaneously in different countries? Independent original invention is declining in a world as connected as ours. It is the creativity of execution that is unique.

Would Wozniak's invention of the Macintosh today be able to be as original as it was when it was first developed? Probably not. There would likely be too much chatter of similar inventions.

At the time it did however impress Bill Gates, "To create a new standard, it takes something that's not just a little bit different; it takes something that's really new and really captures people's imagination, and the Macintosh, of all the machines I've ever seen, is the only one that meets that standard."

The Warning of "Atlas Shrugged"

The answer to the question of the previous chapter – *One idea vs thousands?* – is now most definitely the multitude of creative decisions required for implementation. If we don't start recognizing the work of the execution creatives who change our world, they will walk away leaving the world to lesser performers. Then where would we be. Ideas without execution. The warnings of "Atlas Shrugged" might become a reality.

"Atlas Shrugged" is a science fiction book by Ayn Rand (1957) which has now become a movie trilogy (2011, 2012, 2014). According to Harriet Rubin's 2007 article in the New York Times, Rand's stated goal for writing the novel was "to show how desperately the world needs prime movers and how viciously it treats them" and to portray "what happens to a world without them."

According to Steve Wozniak, "One of the final films Jobs saw was Part 1 of "Atlas Shrugged" at his local theater. Steve was very fast thinking and wanted to do things, I wanted to build things. I think "Atlas Shrugged" was one of his guides in life."

This classic novel depicts the economic carnage caused by big government run amok. The mistakes of patent law (BlackBerry) and contract and intellectual property law (Facebook) impede the success of the very entrepreneurial work they are designed to protect.

Humanity needs the facility to adapt, create, innovate, and execute. So why allow people who have nothing to offer on this front to destroy those who are proven worldchangers? BlackBerry's success is no more. The brilliant expansionist, Jim Balsillie, is no longer catalyzing world advance. Inventor Mike Lazaridis has been sidelined.

And don't get me started on the antitrust case in which the U.S. government accused Microsoft of illegally maintaining a monopoly position in the PC market. Is this what we want? Ayn Rand's warning might come true. *The greats will shrug and walk away*.

18

Assume Nonlinear Progression

P eople assume greatness comes from linearly pursuing one's goals with unwavering focus. That is not the case with savanting. One of the hardest adjustments that needs to be made for embracing the new savant-inspired protocol is the shift to a nonlinear modus operandi.

The biological mechanisms you'll be exploiting operate nonlinearly so you likely will seldom know where you are going or even which of your goals the bioflow is facilitating at any point in time. If you want to truly embrace the power of partnering with internal and external biology, you'll need to release the idea of linear progression.

Accordingly, there are a few nonlinear situations I want to highlight for you: (a) living by leaps, (b) a savanting growth path, (c) *savant-domain side ventures for growth and/or creations*, and (d) integration into global trends. If you know nature's intent and direction, it will be easier to exploit the ever-re-maximizing and ever-advancing biological infrastructure of which we are a part.

Advancing by nonlinear quantum leaps

Nature is nonlinear because, first, it is faster or second, it may not be possible to achieve an adaptation or creation linearly. Consider the evolution of the human eye, for example. It is more likely that existing successful eye mechanisms were re-combined for a quantum leap to a working eye than that each part was evolved linearly.

Evolution proceeds by quantum leaps. Therefore, when you partner with nature's maximizing machinery, your progress will be nonlinear quantum leaps. Breakthroughs, epiphanies, flashes of genius, and clusters of coincidences are all quantum leaps. They are nonlinear because where you end up post-leap may not be a linear projection from where you started pre-leap.

Leaps can bypass hundreds of linear steps at a time to help you to achieve your goals faster. Quantum leap living is therefore highly desirable. You'll want to release yourself from demanding linear progression so that you can be taken to the right information at the right time for these leaps.

Over time, you'll come to know the telltale of the advance of the bioflow maximizing machinery so that you know that you are moving in the right direction even though you may not know precisely where the bioflow is taking you. Living life by leaps will then not be as unnerving.

Steve Jobs agrees with a breakthrough way of life: "I have a great respect for incremental improvement, and I've done that sort of thing in my life, but I've always been attracted to the more revolutionary changes. I don't know why. Because they're harder. They're much more stressful emotionally. And you usually go through a period where everybody tells you that you've completely failed."

Your nonlinear growth path

Savanting is about complying with the pressure of the bioflow externally and internal drives and biochemistry to operate at one's maximum. As such, it is about enhancing the application of one's core strengths and talents. One cannot sustain one's maximum if one grows along a linear path from point A to point B or from one set of capabilities to another.

Therefore, your natural growth path must be an intensification of your biological core. Think in terms of expanding concentric circles around your strongest, most rewarding talents. As you expand to each wider concentric circle, your strongest talents and your impact would increase. Thus, your natural growth path is nonlinear. It will require nonlinear quantum leaps to expand to each wider expansion.

Simultaneously, there will be nonlinear quantum leaps to continuously narrow to more precisely express your core essence. Oprah risked her career success multiple times to make these kinds of adjustments. So too did Bill Gates with his departure from Microsoft to a new world of mega-philanthropy.

Side Ventures for savant-domain growth and creations

With savanting one re-combines existing systems to generate new creations and new solutions to your goals; so too does nature acting on us. Nature re-combines us with relevant systems to create a new more adaptive solution or context when we cannot advance our domain linearly.

If (a) you can no longer move to maximization in your current context or (b) your goals change significantly or (c) you need to grow to achieve your goals or (d) you need to create something for your path which cannot be done on your path, then the bioflow will regroup your system with other more appropriate systems or contexts.

Following the usual bioflow signposts to advance in these circumstances may take you to a place that appears outside of your savant domain. However, these *side ventures* are the means to get what you need to take your savant domain to a new level. They appear to be off your natural growth path but they are not. They are a way to accelerate your advance of your savant domain.

Side ventures and their relationship to creativity and growth may be demonstrated admirably through Steve Jobs. Jobs was forced out of Apple in 1985. He was locked out of the pathway that had arisen from his pursuit of the advance of his savant domain in consumer engineering.

Steve admitted, "I didn't see it then, but it turned out that getting fired from Apple was the best thing that could have ever happened to me. The heaviness of being successful was replaced by the lightness of being a beginner again, less sure about everything. It freed me to enter one of the most creative periods of my life."[53]

I suspect that the bureaucracy of Apple had taken Steve out of his savant-domain flow states. Left to himself, he could now return to serial savantflows, serial breakthroughs, serial creative inspirations and flashes of genius, and the joy of Eureka events.

On his *side venture*, Steve started a company called NeXT, Inc. then later, NeXT Computer, Inc. and NeXT Software, Inc. that built workstation computers. Jobs had created a computer platform development company specializing in state-of-the-art, higher-end computers for higher-education and business markets.

In this *side venture*, Steve shifted from a diehard hardware guy to a savvy software expert with some unique strategic innovations. He also built Pixar which brought him into the world of Disney and the opportunity to garner business acumen and strategies from the best.

In 1995, Pixar created the world's first computer-animated feature film, "Toy Story." Steve Jobs was its executive producer. It won numerous awards and was nominated for three Academy

Awards. Pixar became the most successful animation studio in the world. It was acquired by the Walt Disney Company in 2006.

By 1997, Apple was nearly bankrupt. Jobs negotiated Apple's purchase of NeXT for $427 million by demonstrating that its hardware and software innovations could be used in Apple's future products. This enabled him to return as Apple's CEO and bring the company back to profitability by 1998.

In Steve's words, "In a remarkable turn of events, Apple bought NeXT, I returned to Apple, and the technology we developed at NeXT is at the heart of Apple's current renaissance." While it appeared that Steve had left his savant-domain path, he obviously never stopped working on it. He could produce the creations and achieve the personal growth necessary in another context – *in a side venture.*

He had developed key technology which could save Apple that would likely not have been possible from within Apple. His seemingly circuitous route had advanced his savant domain faster and better than if he had remained at Apple.

He had assimilated new technology skills, new management skills, new creations, a new attitude, new confidence, and new acclaim. He had needed a freer context to retool himself and to rethink the technology as the consumer engineering genius that he was.

As a result, Jobs returned to Apple significantly advanced, expanded, upgraded, more impactful, more skilled, and more creative. He had shifted from a pure hardware guy to finesse with software which would empower iTunes and all the wonderful iPod and iPad devices to follow. Having left Apple, Jobs did not wear any of the failures the company suffered during his absence. He was a hero upon his return.

Steve's *side venture* then was essential to accelerating and enhancing his main creative conduit through Apple. With his "Think different" campaign, Jobs began to work on a line of devices that would have larger cultural ramifications: the iMac (1998); iTunes, the Apple Stores, and the iPod (2001); the iTunes Store (2003); the iPhone (2007); the App Store (2008); and the iPad (2010).

Over time, you'll come to trust the biological guidance system that leads you seemingly off-path to these nonlinear *side ventures*. You'll be following the same signals that you do daily but you'll learn to adjust to the fact that they are not taking you along the path you had come to expect.

You'll want to aspire to this continuous creative process as you scale new frontiers in your career. You'll want to move with nature in order to better collide with the right information at the right time to re-combine it into new breakthrough systems and solutions.

Integration into nonlinear global trends

The bioflow can be used as a biological guidance system because it identifies the direction of the evolution of humanity. As such, it will be nonlinear and filled with leaps. Partnering with it will therefore lead you again on a nonlinear path.

Linking to the evolutionary forces advancing civilization is the means to keep careers, companies, and creations leading-edge. From the forefront, one has the best chance of developing commercially viable breakthroughs for the population that is following behind.

This nonlinear biological guidance system gave our superachievers the means to go into unknown territory safely and expeditiously. They knew that they were proceeding in the right direction for each of them and for humanity. We were all born fully integrated into this biological guidance system. Our six superachievers never relinquished their partnership with the bioflow from birth. As they demonstrate, this is the ultimate career strategy for those seeking to be worldchangers and worldbuilders.

Every living organism is fulfilled when it follows the
right path for its own nature.
Marcus Aurelius, *Meditations*

---

[53] Steve Jobs, Commencement address on June 12, 2005, Stanford News https://news.stanford.edu/2005/06/14/jobs-061505/

V

SAVANTING TO MAN'S HIGHEST GOALS

Chapters

19

Savanting Projected

The lives of our six superachiever models have demonstrated many of the capabilities of the savant-inspired protocol. However, when we project out from the foundation presented so far, we discover that savanting is a means to attain many of the life goals shared across humanity.

These life goals have been addressed by religions, spiritual disciplines, psychology and philosophy. Savanting is an entirely new biology-based route for those who aspire to mankind's highest states of being.

It is therefore a means to meet these universal goals for anyone regardless of their religious, spiritual, or cultural beliefs. As such, savanting is a common modus operandi which may cross national and cultural boundaries to unite humanity.

SAVANTING SO FAR

Let's review what we've discovered so far about the savant-inspired protocol before examining the further potential of this new modus operandi. Savanting is a breakthrough in human creativity, ingenuity, and potential. This breakthrough has three related components. First and foremost is the discovery of an internal-external maximizing bioflow machinery which extends human potential beyond the physical limits of what is within us.

When either savants or nonsavants are operating at their biological maximum or progressing towards it, our internal maximizing machinery merges with an external machinery maximizing all living systems with which we have co-evolved to operate. True human potential emerges when we have engaged the entire internal-external evolutionary engine to achieve our goals.

The second discovery is a subset of the first. There is logic and evidence that the massive information behind savant superskills may be externally sourced. This is because, first, current knowledge of deficient savant brains suggest that they cannot exhibit the genius that they do. And second, the mechanisms of their genius have not yet been found. If their genius is externally sourced, then it may be accessible to all of us.

The third discovery is reliant on the first two discoveries. Because we are meant to operate at our maximum, we have evolved a mechanism to instantly click us into our peak performance state. Savantflows.

A savantflow emerges when we are applying out strongest most rewarding constellation of drives and talents to the most meaningful work for the most valuing audience – real or imagined. It also emerges when we are pursuing growth and learning in our savant domains.

In flow, attention is 100% focused on the activity at hand. Peak performance and growth are built in. Time, space, and even self-awareness cease to exist. Flow is intrinsically rewarding. It is an addictive drive that will raise one's baseline functionality over time. It is not surprising that it has been a key catalyst of human evolution.

Your partnership with the bioflow will help you to identify your best cause, purpose, or field of endeavor – your savant domain. It will make creatives of noncreatives and execution creatives from the execution-challenged. The bioflow is an evolutionary guidance system which will empower nonvisionaries to operate as if they have the gift of vision.

There is evidence that when we enter the altered consciousness of savantflow, we may have the same ability to access external information that savants do. Savant brains uncontrolled by left brains and the brains of nonsavants in savantflow may achieve similar states.

To restate this another way, it appears that the damaged brains of savants and the activity-focused flow brains of those of normal intelligence operating in their savant domain both yield savant-like genius.

The resulting inflow of savant-domain information appears to be fuel required for the creativity behind our adaptivity. We have evolved to be creative beings. Spontaneous information is just one of the many supporting mechanisms and processes.

Due to left-brain deficiencies, the creative process may not complete beyond the information fueling stage in savants. This would suggest that creativity is not solely reliant on right-brain activity or more savants would be creative. As it turns out, science has indeed shown that segments from both sides of the brain are involved in creativity.

SAVANTING PROJECTION POTENTIAL

I made an in-depth review of the peak states of many religious, spiritual, philosophical, and psychological disciplines. I discovered that each of their descriptions of advanced states of human consciousness or the evolved states of mankind derive from the belief system to which the speaker from each discipline subscribes. Therefore, peak states called by the same name may not in fact be the same. There is not universal agreement on the meaning of our peak states.

Therefore, I have decided I must compare the projections of savanting to definitions of peak states which more easily allow comparisons with the capabilities of savanting. So, my apologies in advance if the peak goal states I define do not encompass all the definitions to which readers might subscribe. Let's take a closer look at how savanting enables one to achieve these popular goal states in new ways.

20

Enlightenment from Extreme Self-Knowledge

For many, their purpose in life is the discovery of self and how to fully express that self. In fact, one popular definition of enlightenment is "self-knowledge." The Zen term for enlightenment is "kenshō." It means "seeing into one's true nature." Enlightenment in the West has become synonymous with *self-realization* or *self-actualization*.

Here are enlightenment quotes from other sectors: Adyashanti claims "Enlightenment means waking up to what you truly are and then being that." Zen Master Eihei Dogen advises "To study the Buddha Way is to study the self; to study the self is to forget the self; to forget the self is to be enlightened by the ten thousand things."

And, to quote Lao-Tse again: "He who knows others is wise; he who knows himself is enlightened." Lao-Tse, also known as Laozi and Lao Tzu, was an ancient Chinese philosopher and writer. He is the reputed author of the Tao Te Ching, the founder of philosophical Taoism, and a deity in religious Taoism and traditional Chinese religions. Here are some of the comments by Lao-Tse from that revered tome on self-knowledge and enlightenment:

- *When I let go of what I am, I become what I might be.*

- *If you understand others you are smart. If you understand yourself, you are illuminated.*
- *Knowing others is intelligence; knowing yourself is true wisdom. Mastering others is strength; mastering yourself is true power. He who conquers others is strong; he who conquers himself is mighty*
- *Enlightenment of the absolute Tao can free a person from worries and sorrow.*
- *Hope and fear are both phantoms that arise from thinking of the self. When we don't see the self as self, what do we have to fear?*
- *A person of knowledge and self-opinion will be hindered from the enlightenment of Tao.*

HOW SAVANTING INCREASES SELF-KNOWLEDGE

Self-knowledge means that one can shape one's life to reflect one's true self. One might then change the world full throttle from one's essence. The savanting modus operandi is essentially driven by the creative self-expression of your true essence – your maximum biological predisposition as determined by the bioflow.

As a result, by following the protocol, you'll know yourself and the ideal purpose and direction of your life. You'll "know" what you came here to do even if you cannot put words around it. You'll be doing activities in savantflows which not only express your essence but reinforce it – which nourish you and make you more than you have ever been before.

This self-knowledge will eliminate many potential missteps and provide the means for greater sure-footedness in directing your life. Most people crave this information.

Activities theme inciting past bioflow support

Extreme self-knowledge cannot be discovered by personality, function, or skill tests and assessments. Years of meditation and introspection may not provide you with what you might learn right now today by simply discovering the theme of activities which invoked bioflow support in your past.

A clustering of internal and external leaps triggered by the bioflow will reveal what "nature" considers your biological maximum: your strongest talents; what you are passionate about; what is meaningful to you; and, ultimately, your savant domain – your best territory for your most meaningful, contributory, rewarding work. You'll even know which projects will and won't work in the future based on your past experience.

Look for the pattern in the types of activities which caused internal leaps such as breakthroughs, epiphanies, and flashes of genius. Then look for a theme in the activities which triggered external leaps such as clusters of coincidences, models, and facilitating people and events externally. These indicate activities which the bioflow supports.

Past bioflow support predicts future support. This is because your maximum is a constant and how the bioflow attempts to maximize your system is a constant. These constants reveal extreme knowledge about your past, present, and future.

As a corollary, the greater your self-knowledge, the easier it will be to operate at your maximum in order to merge with the surrounding bio-infrastructure with which we have co-evolved to operate. Your capabilities, resources, functionality, and potential will be extended to speed goal achievement. To court the magic of the bioflow, you'll have determined from themes of past events the knowledge, learning, growth and creativity you crave and the frontiers you would choose to scale.

You'll also know your growth path to new functionality and expanded impact that the bioflow will be pressuring you to pursue – your expansion by concentric circles around your core strengths, talents, and passions and the constellation of drives, emotions, and biochemistry pulling you to the creative self-expression of your essence. Complying with the savanting protocol reveals a lot of information about yourself that most never learn.

Self-knowledge from your savant domain

You'll have discovered a savant domain through which you could perfectly express your true self. How much more do we know about Oprah Winfrey when you connect a continuum from her natural draw to recite sermons at ages three and four to what she has pursued through her career until now. The continuity of her drives tells you much more about her than her biography.

The same with Jeff Bezos. Draw a savant domain from the young boy addicted to science fiction books about worldbuilding, a dream of colonization in space, and continuous experimentation in his garage with respect to new frontiers.

Suddenly you know why he chose entrepreneurial firms with large global systems in New York's financial district. You know why he pursued the global spread of Amazon through frontier after frontier into new fields. You'll understand why he set up Blue Origin to develop spaceships for the colonization of space. And you'll understand his investment personally and through Amazon in companies that are dedicated to his vision of worldbuilding.

Our understanding of Mark Zuckerberg also increases with knowledge of his savant domain. Think of the young boy who was inspired in so many ways to build relationships among family and friends. Zucknet, for example, an intranet for his family, an instant chat system, a conduit for playing games and sharing music, all of which built bonds. Then the building of relationships at school after school globally until Facebook went global. And then on to building relationships to address social needs wherever they arise in the world.

Do you see the relationship theme of Mark's life? Do you now know why a programming prodigy would take psychology at Harvard? Do you know the future advance of Zuckerberg's savant domain? Can you predict his future?

The same goes for the other icons. You can see how well you can know the inner drives of complete strangers by tracking their savant domain. You can see the directions that the bioflow will favor for them. Imagine what you'll come to know about yourself simply by getting into savantflows day after day and year after year.

How many people have craved this knowledge? How much easier everyone's life would be if they discovered their own formula for moving with their natural maximization path and the evolutionary flow of the world rather than fighting against them.

What could you accomplish if you spent decades focused only on the application and growth of your strongest talents in your savant domain operating continuously beyond your potential through partnering with the maximizing machinery? If we removed all restrictions and provided you with every freedom and resource, what could the "maximized you" accomplish?

Self-knowledge from flow

Savanting increases self-knowledge because it is based on serial savantflows. Here is what flow expert Csikszentmihalyi has to say about ordinary flow and self-knowledge: "After an episode of flow is over, we generally emerge from it with a stronger self-concept; we know that we have succeeded in meeting a difficult challenge. We might even feel that we have stepped out of the boundaries of the ego and have become part, at least temporarily, of a larger entity.

"The musician feels at one with the harmony of the cosmos, the athlete moves at one with the team, the reader of a novel lives for a few hours in a different reality. Paradoxically, the self expands through acts of self-forgetfulness."[54]

Self-knowledge from your "Personbook"

In chapter 6, I introduced the concept of downloading whole systems of information from the bioflow in the form of "personbooks," "factbooks," and "procedurebooks." You may recall that one example of "personbooks" was demonstrated by the various personalities expressed in those with multiple personality disorder whereby each personality had information never sourced by the MPD patient through his/her five senses.

I previously suggested that one could theoretically access one's own "personbook" and have sudden spontaneous self-knowledge. This would mean sudden enlightenment. Many have experienced just such events in which they not only thoroughly understood themselves but also why they were here. What their mission must be.

Often these sudden enlightenment events are clothed in knowledge of suddenly understanding how the universe operates so that they may apply it to that mission. There is a feeling of being home that few experience. Those who have experienced it spend their lives trying to return to that comforting but wondrous expansion.

For some, extreme self-knowledge is their goal. This goal will obviously be met by savanting. However, savanting may also be the answer for those seeking other life goals such as self-love, happiness, wholeness, self-actualization, self-transcendence, purpose and even cosmic consciousness.

Self-sufficient sustainable self-love

Many have spent their lives seeking love. They have sought someone to complete them. Savanting offers a more satisfying goal – self-sufficient, sustainable, self-love. Savanting exploits evolution's goals. Evolution has selected for the human system a multitude of mechanisms to entice us to operate at our maximum to change our realities with creations, creativity, and creative expressions of our essence.

If you were evolution, would you not have built such a powerful constellation of emotions into the maximum modus operandi you wanted to reinforce? This emotional cocktail is what makes savant-domain activities intrinsically rewarding for our six icons. They were not driven by external rewards.

We've evolved a constellation of rewarding emotions and drives to addict us to creative self-expressions which imprint the world in the way in which we have been biologically predisposed. Complying with this constellation entices us to make mark the world with our most meaningful, most passionate work.

Always this includes self-esteem. But, more than this, self-love is embedded in the creative work we do in our savantflows. You may not have realized that "self-love" was the emotion you were experiencing in your savantflows. However, you have no doubt observed this self-love in others.

Have you ever watched someone speak passionately about their lifework from a flow state? A singer lost in the emotion of a song? A motivational speaker carried away by their own inspirational message and the love they feel for their audience? A CEO moved by her passion for a product resulting from years of serial savantflows?

This is the moment they are experiencing self-love. It is so palpable that even an outsider can feel it. This is an emotional state sustainable by a serial-savantflow lifestyle. We are biochemically wired for self-love from creative self-expression.

When I asked myself why evolution would have selected for this draw to creative self-expression, it seemed to me that this was another proof that we have evolved to be creative beings. Suddenly the whole spontaneous knowledge of savants made sense.

Savants have the information inflow portion of the creative process – the fuel for the re-combining of existing information to create new information systems. This is as you would expect if we are meant to maximize around constantly producing creations or changes to the world to express our essence.

However, you will learn shortly that creativity has been discovered to be a whole-brain process rather than a right-brain process as originally thought. Since savants have damaged left brains they are, in many cases, unable to complete the second stage of the creative process for which they attracted the massive information inflow behind their savant superskills.

This is further reinforcement that each of us is likely wired by evolution for this information fuel inflow and eventually savantflows become deep enough to turn on and turn off the parts of our brain to duplicate the damaged savant brain. The fact that studies show that our creativity increases in flow state seems to reinforce our biological predisposition for both the first and the second stages of the creative process.

---

[54] Mihalyi Csikszentmihalyi, *Creativity: Flow and the psychology of discovery and invention*, 1997b, New York: HarperCollins Publishers., p. 112-113

21

Self-Actualization and Self-Transcendence

Your own Self-Realization is the greatest service you can render the world. Ramana Maharshi

We are conscious beings always experimenting with the mystery of becoming our ultimate manifestation.
Kilroy J. Oldster, *Dead Toad Scrolls*

Upon entering into the divine domain of transcendence, all these religious founders truly felt that they had accessed the true meaning of the universe, while in reality, what they had access to, in that state of mind, was their inner self.
Abhijit Naskar

As human beings we are made to surpass ourselves and are truly ourselves only when transcending ourselves. Huston Smith

Self-Actualization through savanting

Self-actualization is another goal that many are pursuing which may be more easily achieved through savanting. Self-actualization is the process by which an individual reaches full potential. It entails the ongoing actualization of potentials, capacities, and talents.

Abraham Maslow, the American psychologist and philosopher who coined the term, defines it this way: "[Self-actualization] refers to the person's desire for self-fulfillment, namely, to the tendency for him to become actualized in what he is potentially."[55] "The job is, if we are willing to take it seriously, to help ourselves to be more perfectly what we are, to be more full, more actualizing, more realizing, in fact, what we are in potentiality." "Think of self-actualization as the need to become what one has the potential to be."

This is another intrinsically rewarding endeavor which many might better pursue through savanting. Maslow states that one realizes this potential for its own gratification – not for any external gain or concern of what others will think or say.

Additional comments by Maslow about self-actualization:

- *Self-actualizing people must be what they can be.*
- *What a man can be, he must be. This need we call self-actualization.*
- *One's only rival is one's own potentialities. One's only failure is failing to live up to one's own possibilities. In this sense, every man can be a king, and must therefore be treated like a king.*
- *A musician must make music, an artist must paint, a poet must write, if he is to be ultimately at peace with himself.*
- *All the evidence that we have indicates that it is reasonable to assume in practically every human being, and certainly in almost every newborn baby, that there is an active will toward health, an impulse towards growth, or towards the actualization.*
- *Self-actualizing people have a deep feeling of identification, sympathy, and affection for human beings in general. They feel kinship and connection as if all people were members of a single family.*
- *One cannot choose wisely for a life unless he dares to listen to himself, his own self, at each moment of his life.*

In case you hadn't yet realized it, self-actualization is a byproduct of savanting. In fact, access to our internal-external potential undoubtedly exceeds whatever peak state Maslow had envisioned. Savanting's requirement for maximization to conscript the resources of the surrounding bio-infrastructure implies operating at your full potential. In more colloquial terms, it enables the pursuit of one's calling.

It entails applying your strongest most rewarding talents to the most meaningful, intrinsically or biologically rewarding activities. It is about exploiting your biological predisposition to the maximum. One's greatest intrinsic regards will inevitably lead to one's greatest extrinsic rewards over and above experiencing the most sought-after emotional highs.

In 1943, Maslow developed his famous *Needs Hierarchy Theory*. It proposes that human beings have a set of needs that need to be fulfilled hierarchically in order to be free to pursue self-actualization.

According to Maslow, human needs progress up a hierarchy from physiological to safety to belongingness and love, to esteem, and finally to self-actualization. This respected framework is used extensively in research and education in various fields like sociology, management, psychology, psychiatry, and such.

However, by the time of his book, "Farther Reaches of Human Nature," published in 1971, Maslow had realized what you have already learned from studying the six superachievers presented in this book. The savanting goal state is so biologically compelling that all the needs in Maslow's hierarchy are bypassed in favor of pursuing self-actualization directly.[56]

We have seen from our six superachievers and from our own life experiences that people will forego the lower needs in Maslow's hierarchy if they can go into savantflow invoked by the work they love.

For example, think of programmers working through the night without food or sleep. Or starving artists who cannot leave their painting to address physical needs. Think of gamers who have found the perfect game which so captivates them that it's hours before they can stop.

In his breakthrough book, "Flow: The Psychology of Optimal Experience" (1990), Csikszentmihalyi describes flow as "a state in which people are so involved in an activity that nothing else seems to matter; the experience is so enjoyable that people will continue to do it even at great cost, for the sheer sake of doing it."

Maslow came to view self-actualized people as being driven by what he named "metamotivation." Rather than seeking fulfillment of basic needs such as food, sleep, safety and self-esteem, they are driven to fulfill their full potential at all costs. He proved this theory by studying individuals like Albert Einstein, Henry David Thoreau, Ruth Benedict, and others whom he believed had achieved self-actualization.

Maslow stated that people who are self-actualizing and driven by metamotivation "are dedicated people, devoted to some task 'outside themselves,' some vocation, or duty, or beloved job." Maslow further explains that a calling could be construed as a destiny or fate and that such people are particularly talented in their field and could be called "naturals."

I don't limit self-actualization to "naturals" as Maslow does. Rather, I believe that everyone has a biologically maximum state – savantflows within a savant domain – in which they can self-actualize – in which they can apply their strongest most rewarding talents to achieve at their full potential. We have seen this even with savants with damaged left brains. Savanting is a viable route for those seeking an accelerated path to self-actualization.

197

Self-transcendence through savanting

Many have sought self-transcendence through religious, spiritual, philosophical or psychological prescriptions and disciplines. Savanting offers a secular, biology-maximizing protocol to not only more quickly and more naturally achieve the same ends but to sustain them.

In savanting's savantflows, the states of self-actualization and self-transcendence are biology-based and thus are integrated rather than hierarchical.

Csikszentmihalyi finds that flow state is fertile territory for self-transcendence, "When not preoccupied with our selves, we actually have a chance to expand the concept of who we are. Loss of self-consciousness can lead to self-transcendence, to a feeling that the boundaries of our being have been pushed forward."[57] "The self expands through acts of self forgetfulness."

Initially, I assumed self-transcendence would be about surpassing ourselves as Csikszentmihalyi suggests. It represented growth to me. However, other psychologists define it with another dimension. Viktor Frankl,[58] Abraham Maslow,[59] Pamela G. Reed,[60] C. Robert Cloninger and Lars Tornstam, for example, have made contributions to what has become a theory of self-transcendence.

Pamela Reed's Self Transcendence Theory defines self-transcendence as an "increased awareness of dimensions greater than the self and expansions of personal boundaries within intrapersonal, interpersonal, transpersonal, and temporal domains."[61]

Self-actualization goals are self-focused and self-serving. Self-transcendence goals are other-focused. For self-actualization, an individual seeks fulfillment of personal potential. For self-transcendence, one seeks to further a cause beyond the self.

Self-actualization refers to one becoming one's "best self." Self-transcendence refers to improving and/or being of service to the world as a whole. It's about making a difference in the grand scheme of things. It entails transcending or rising above the self to relate to that which is greater than the self.

According to Reed and her colleagues, self-transcendence shifts us from the instinctive selfishness of self-actualization to a state of selflessness. It expands our personal boundaries to that which is greater than the self. It is the realization that you are one small part of a greater whole.

It is about the humanitarianism we observed in our six superachievers right from childhood and the commitment of their companies and careers to products and services that *benefit individuals en masse*. I attributed this to the bioflow simultaneously maximizing the individual and the species.

For many years, self-actualization dominated Maslow's famous Hierarchy of Needs. He considered self-actualization the pinnacle of human development and the highest human need. The realization of one's full potential is indeed a lofty goal of development. However, self-transcendence is the "next level" of development. It focuses on things beyond the self like altruism, spiritual awakening, liberation from egocentricity, and the unity of being.

Maslow equated this with the desire to reach the infinite. He described it as "a larger-than-life experience of self-realization characterized by a mix of spiritual emotions like enlightenment, awe, reverence, humility, happiness, wonder, and connection to the universe, among others."[62]

Maslow increasingly became convinced that *self-actualization is healthy self-realization on the path to self-transcendence.* He felt that the self only finds its actualization in giving itself to some higher outside goal in altruism and spirituality. Perhaps he was influenced by Viktor Frankl's criticism of his work.

Frankl had criticized Maslow for making self-actualization a necessary condition for self-transcendence. In his famous book, "Man's Search for Meaning," Viktor Frankl writes: "… the real aim of human existence cannot be found in what is called self-actualization. Human existence is essentially self-transcendence rather than self-actualization.

Self-actualization is not a possible aim at all; for the simple reason that the more a man would strive for it, the more he would miss it. For only to the extent to which man commits himself to the fulfillment of his life's meaning, to this extent he also actualizes himself. In other words, self-actualization cannot be attained if it's made an end in itself, but only as a side-effect of self-transcendence."[63]

Biology-Driven Self-Actualization and Self-Transcendence

The savanting protocol is based on maximizing one's biology. Your maximization would require you to pursue the most meaningful application of your strongest most rewarding talents. This meets the definition of self-actualization.

In addition, maximizing your system will automatically merge you with the evolutionary bioflow. The bioflow is designed to maximize all living systems – not just yours. If you're merged with the bioflow maximizing machinery, you're going to be maximized in ways which will simultaneously contribute to the maximizing of humanity. Evolutionary forces would always pursue that strategy.

Therefore, self-actualization and self-transcendence are integrated to become a single foundational dynamic of savanting. Together, they are the inevitable byproduct of the savant-inspired protocol. Their integration will become more obvious as one advances one's savant domain and the benefits of one's work become more impactful to the world.

This integration is demonstrated by the worldchanging work of our six superachievers as they pursued intrinsically rewarding activities of self-expression. For most of their lives they have operated from this biological purity. What appeared to be moral, ethical, or philanthropic motivations in fact emerged naturally from biological imperatives that have evolved over generations for the survival of the individual and the species.

The argument as to whether self-actualization must be achieved before self-transcendence is thus moot. It is not meaningful to pursue self-actualization and self-transcendence separately since they both emerge from biological maximization through savanting.

Internally Driven versus Externally Driven

Notice that savanting's self-transcendence is an *internally driven* biological approach. It therefore stands in stark contrast to the prevailing *externally driven* strategies, rules, advice, and teachings for transcending oneself. There are a plethora of religious, spiritual, psychological, behavioral, moral and ethical disciplines, processes, and procedures insisting that self-transcendence is only achievable through *selflessly* serving others.

This has proven not to be the case with our six superachievers. Rather, self-transcendence through savanting emerges through *selfishly* pursuing the work or creative self-expression of one's essence to which one's system is biologically biased. It is achieved by being drawn to activities in one's savant domain that are intrinsically rewarding.

Self-transcendence emerges from complying with the innate drives, the draw of emotional highs, the addictive pull of savantflows, and being guided and accelerated by the magic of coincidences and facilitating events that emerge from partnering with the bioflow. These are mechanisms which have evolved over generations to entice all of us to operate at our maximum. They have evolved to entice us to create, innovate, and impact the world from full strength.

Disciplining oneself to do philanthropic things will therefore fail for most people as the means to self-transcend. But, more importantly, one will absolutely be prevented from self-actualizing. One cannot sacrifice one's potentialities in the service of others. Therefore, pursuing self-transcendence by traditional externally driven means will eliminate the possibility of self-actualization.

Again, with savanting, one does not have to choose either self-actualization or self-transcendence as a goal. They will be the inevitable byproducts of a serial-savantflow way of life.

> *People were more likely to succeed if, instead of believing in a distinction between themselves and the world, and seeing individual people and things as isolated and divisible, they viewed everything as a connected continuum of interactions – and also if they understood that there were other ways to communicate than through the usual channels.*[64]

> William G. Braud, American psychologist and parapsychologist, director of research in parapsychology at the Mind Science Foundation. Professor at the Institute of Transpersonal Psychology

[55] Abraham H. Maslow, *A Theory of Human Motivation*. 1943, Psychological Review, pp. 382–383

[56] *Abraham H. Maslow, "Farther Reaches of Human Nature," 1971, The Viking Press*

[57] Mihaly Csikszentmihalyi, *Flow: The Psychology of Happiness* 1992, Ebury Publishing, Nov. 15, 2013

[58] Frankl, Viktor E. (1966). *Self-transcendence as a human phenomenon. Journal of Humanistic Psychology*, 6, 97–106.

[59] Koltko-Rivera, Mark E. *Rediscovering the later version of Maslow's hierarchy of needs: Self-transcendence and opportunities for theory*, research, and unification. (2006), *Review of General Psychology* 10(4), 302–317.

[60] Reed, P. G.. *Toward a nursing theory of self-transcendence: Deductive reformulation using developmental theories.* 1991, *Advances in Nursing Science*, 13(4), 64–77.

[61] Valerie Lander McCarthy, Jiying Ling, Robert M. Carini, The role of self-transcendence: a missing variable in the pursuit of successful aging? 2013, *p. 179.* University of Louisville, valerie.mccarthy@louisville.edu http://ir.library.louisville.edu/faculty/18

[62] Abraham H. Maslow, *Religions, Values and Peak-Experiences*. (1964). Columbus, OH: Ohio State University Press.

[63] *Man's Search for Meaning* by Viktor E. Frankl, 1959, 1962, 1984, 1992, 2006. First published in German in 1946. The original English title was *From Death-Camp to Existentialism.*

[64] Braud William G. (1975) *PSI-Conducive States.* Journal of Communication 25(1): 142-152.

22

Enlightenment from Flow

We have explored the application of savanting to the achievement of one definition of the enlightenment goal already, that of extreme self-knowledge. There is another category of enlightenment definitions held by many factions which is based on expansions of consciousness. These circles define enlightenment in terms of unity consciousness, oneness, and nonduality.

This second enlightenment goal may also be achieved more quickly and more reliably through savanting. Ever deepening savantflows as one scales frontier after frontier in one's savant domain should achieve the altered states of consciousness sought for enlightenment.

There have not yet been comparative studies done on those in savantflow versus regular flow. However, there is sufficient data collected about flow to indicate that the altered awareness of flow can lead to the states of consciousness promoted by many religions, meditation, and spirituality disciplines.

Accounts of flow bear a striking resemblance to spiritual, ecstatic, and meditative states. The proposed serial-savantflow protocol therefore offers a new approach for those aspiring to this second category of enlightenment.

To set the stage for those pursuing this second enlightenment goal, let me quote myself from *Peak Evolution*'s introduction to flow:

"People stop being aware of themselves as separate from the actions they are performing in flow. They lose all self-consciousness and self-awareness. There is a quantum leap from duality to oneness. The doer and the action are no longer separate. Interconnectedness with all things replaces separation and fragmentation.

This is reminiscent of the Zen idea of no-mind: a state of complete absorption in what one is doing. In Zen, the word for 'mind' and 'the consciousness of the universe' are the same. The mind of the individual and the mind of the universe are also perceived as one in flow."[65]

Beyond self-actualization and self-transcendence

This quote indicates that even in 2001 I had experienced a state of being beyond self-transcendence through my use of the serial savantflows of savanting. I therefore know of what I speak. However, for those seeking this form of enlightenment, reason can also reveal this truth.

Flow is an egoless or *identityless* state of altered awareness generated by activity fusion. Self-actualization and self-transcendence, however, both require us to retain our identity. Savantflow is therefore a peak state which is unrelated to either self-actualization or self-transcendence.

Think about the definitions of self-actualization and self-transcendence proposed by Maslow, Frankl, and others. Notice that they assume you know who you are. One must have self-awareness to realize one's potential. Also, there must be a sense of self in order to serve others or promote causes bigger than oneself. *Duality is assumed.*

Self-actualization and self-transcendence are therefore *identity-required states.* Savanting is driven by flow states. Savantflows are *identityless,* nondual states of consciousness. However, savantflows are different than regular flows. A savantflow emerges from operating at your biological maximum as in self-actualization.

In savantflow, the activity driving the change in your consciousness is an expression of the essence of your system. This activity relates to the application of your strongest most rewarding talent constellation to your most meaningful work. Therefore, this activity *must* be on the path to actualizing your potential. In fact, this activity likely is an expression of you already actualized – already operating at your full potential.

Operating in savantflow attaches the guidance and resources of the bioflow for the activity on which you are focused. It also merges one with the goals of the bioflow which is intent on the survival of the species. Therefore, the activities underlying savantflow lead to self-transcendence in benefiting others for those who believe in that definition of self-transcendence.

Because one must be stretching to do work beyond one's capabilities to launch flow, it is a growth state. Savantflows will therefore invoke self-transcendence to achieve its alternate definition of "surpassing oneself."

We saw both definitions achieved by our six superachievers since childhood. The activities driving their savantflows were dedicated to benefiting humanity. Their success came from *selfishly* doing the work/play that was intrinsically rewarding which, with the guidance of the bioflow, scaled new frontiers to benefit our world.

Self-transcendence emerged from their work long before they each established *unselfish* philanthropic goals.

The savanting modus operandi thus enables one to experience self-actualization, self-transcendence, enlightenment through self-knowledge, and enlightenment through the altered states of consciousness available in deep flow.

THE BIOLOGY OF FLOW

Flow states have been shown to offer the altered states of consciousness and awareness that are pursued by other means through religions and such. This is to be expected since the neuroscience of physical self-dissolution has determined that they all share very unusual patterns of brain activity. Mystical experience, peak experience, and flow are all psychological processes related to transcendent emotions.[66]

Creativity increases in flow

Creativity is greatly increased in flow. One reason is because a phenomenon called "transient hypofrontality" deactivates parts of the prefrontal cortex (PFC). The sense of self created by the PFC therefore disappears. We are freed from interference with creativity due to the silencing of our "inner critic" when the dorsolateral PFC quiets. The subconscious mind then becomes the primary information processor.

A rush of neurotransmitters – such as endorphins, dopamine, norepinephrine, serotonin, oxytocin, and others that increase neuroplasticity – augment one's capabilities in flow. All these neurochemicals are pleasure-inducing, performance-enhancing, and, most importantly to our cause, catalytic to creativity. This is a second reason why creativity is enhanced in flow.

These chemicals and transmitters enable your brain to more rapidly rewire its constituent neuronal connections. Learning accelerates. Memory improves. Knowledge and skill acquisition are two to five times faster during flow. Anandamide increases lateral thinking. One has access to a larger database for search by one's pattern-recognition system.

But, most wonderfully for those pursuing enlightenment through flow, these chemicals flood the system to create a blissful euphoria – a high unlike any other available to us and possibly more addictive.

Unfortunately, these chemicals deplete and need to be replenished. As a result, most flow states are temporary. Enhanced learning only happens in short bursts. Yet we have seen with our six icons that their lives have been replete with serial savantflows of some duration. How is that possible?

> *Contrary to what we usually believe . . . the best*
> *moments in our lives, are not the passive, receptive,*
> *relaxing times . . . The best moments usually occur*
> *when a person's body or mind is stretched to its*
> *limits in a voluntary effort to accomplish something*
> *difficult and worthwhile. Optimal experience*
> *[(flow)] is thus something that we make happen.*[67]
> Mihaly Csikszentmihalyi

Sustainable self-transcendent flow

Surprisingly, there is one kind of flow which has been studied that is not subject to neurotransmitter exhaustion. *Altruistic flow* or *self-transcendent flow*. We experience an emotional or biochemical high when we are doing things for others.

Accordingly, an altruistic flow can extend for a couple of days. This suggests the kind of chronic state of flow that we see in the lives of our six superachievers. It shows that it is scientifically possible to remain in a peak state of consciousness for extended periods of time.

Evolution is predictable in evolving mechanisms to ensure the survival of the individual and the species. Altruism benefits the species. Evolution has therefore selected mechanisms to make altruistic flow compelling and addictive to give us a survival advantage. Altruism is the most reliable trigger of long-lasting flow states and the activation of peak performance and human potential.

Self-transcendent flow in our six icons

Altruistic or self-transcendent flow is the very type of flow we observed in the lives of our six superachievers. Their savant domains were dedicated to benefiting humanity long before they had the financial wherewithal to become significant philanthropists. This gives us an explanation for the lengthy flow states of our six superachievers. Therefore, this might serve as further confirmation that savanting was their shared formula for success.

Think of the goals of Amazon, Facebook, Apple, Microsoft. Each benefitted humanity while being the means for each founder to make his living doing the work he found intrinsically rewarding.

Oprah's serial savantflows during her long interviews were driven by her need to help people. Her life has been a quest for knowledge to be shared with large audiences to better the lives of the masses. Her voracious reading also generated her serial-savantflow way of life adding to her experience of self-knowledge, self-actualization, self-transcendence, and enlightenment.

Jim Carrey's savantflows during his acting or entertaining were driven by his need to uplift the spirits of audiences. Jeff Bezos experiences serial savantflows when inventing and creating for planetary and galactic expansion to improve the quality of life of individuals *en masse*.

Bill Gates continues the serial savantflows and savant domain that built Microsoft, its products, its industry, its market and civilization into the field of mega-philanthropy where he builds the missions and infrastructure to improve the quality of life of whole segments of the planet's population. Mark Zuckerberg continues his global relationship-building to benefit his social missions.

The hack modes of Gates, Zuckerberg and Bezos to build products and services improved quality of life across the globe. Steve Jobs' experienced self-transcendent savantflows for his breakthrough consumer design work and his charismatic promotional speeches. His last act on earth was to have the "Autobiography of the Yogi" distributed at his funeral.

Again, let me reiterate that each of the six was simply pursuing intrinsically rewarding activities that were internally driven. They were not complying with external rules or pressures to become philanthropic as are embedded within so many of our cultural constructs.

Their philanthropy was biology-driven by complying with the goals of the bioflow. In addition, beneficial mechanisms have evolved over generations within the human biochemistry driving savantflows within one's savant domain to help the individual and the species to survive and thrive.

Flow formula for enlightenment

We now have our formula for sustainable enlightenment through flow. *It is a formula based on serial savantflows generated by intrinsically rewarding activities for which one is most biological predisposed.* These activities will come to have socially beneficial purposes on their own or when the bioflow merges during savantflows.

A compelling cycle of serial self-transcendence is built into this formula. Flow states are inherently peak-growth, peak-performance states because one must be stretched beyond one's previous capabilities in order to invoke them. The altered states of awareness inherent in flow states are enhanced in savantflows which express one's biology-based essence. More significant expansions of consciousness are consequently more prevalent.

This would explain why, upon closer examination, it seems that most religions and spiritual disciplines have anchored their instructions for experiencing enlightenment around an altruistic flow trigger. Savantflows incite similar no-self and nondual awarenesses when initiated by savant-domain activities.

However, note that the two definitions of enlightenment prevalent in society are in conflict yet both are met by savanting. One form of enlightenment emerges from the dissolution of self in flow. The other emerges from the extreme self-knowledge that emerges as one pursues self-actualization and self-transcendence. Serial savantflows may be the fastest most predictable route to experiencing the most advanced states of being.

> *In unity consciousness, in no-boundary awareness,*
> *the sense of self expands to totally include everything*
> *once thought to be not-self. One's sense of identity*
> *shifts to the entire universe, to all worlds, high or*
> *low, manifest or unmanifest, sacred or profane. And*
> *obviously this cannot occur as long as the primary*
> *boundary, which separates the self from the universe,*
> *is mistaken as real.* Ken Wilber

[65]   Lauren Holmes, 2001/2010, *Peak Evolution: Beyond Peak Performance and Peak Experience, Chapter 14*, Beyond Flow: Egolessness, Nonduality and Oneness

[66]   Yaden, D. B., Iwry, J., Slack, K. J., Eichstaedt, J. C., Zhao, Y., Vaillant, G. E., et al. (2016). The overview effect: Awe and self-transcendence experience in space flight. *Theory Res. and Pract.* 3, 1–11. doi: 10.1037/cns0000086

[67]   Mihaly Csikszentmihalyi, *Flow: The Psychology of Happiness* 1992, Ebury Publishing, November 15, 2013

23

Awe and Wholeness

Not only do self-actualization and self-transcendence emerge from the savantflows driving savanting, but so too does another oft-pursued goal – "awe." This is the emotion which attracts so many to religious and spiritual organizations. It even draws extraterrestrial believers to the UFO "religion."

Awe is a powerfully addictive emotion. Awe experiences are innately self-transcendent. They shift our attention away from ourselves. They make us feel as if we are part of something greater than ourselves. They make us more generous toward others.

The 2003 paper of Keltner and Haidt,[68] "Approaching Awe – A Moral, Spiritual, and Aesthetic Emotion," identifies studies which show that awe is often accompanied by feelings of self-diminishment and increased connectedness with other people. Experiencing awe often puts people in a self-transcendent state where they focus less on themselves and more on being part of a larger whole.

In this way, awe is both an altered state of consciousness and an emotional state. As such, it is akin to flow state.[69] In fact, awe is a component of the addictive draw of flow.

Shiota et al. (2007) define awe as "an emotional response to perceptually vast stimuli that overwhelm current mental structures yet facilitate attempts at accommodation."

Awe is one of the very rare emotions that turn our minds outwards rather than inwards. The experience of awe entices us to transcend the boundaries of our individual self. We are drawn outside of ourselves to wonder at phenomena in the natural world, the noble actions of others, or the genius of creativity. Our daily concerns and ingrained expectations of life are revised as a result.

Another consequence of the "diminished sense of self" spawned by awe is an enhanced awareness of being part of something infinitely larger and more universal. Shiota et al. (2007) report that those asked to re-live an awe-inspiring moment revealed pronounced feelings of love, connectedness to the world around them, rapture, contentment, awareness of something greater than the self, a lack of awareness of everyday concerns, and a desire to prolong the emotional state for as long as possible.[70]

Awe is a compelling part of the beneficial addiction to the savant-inspired protocol once you start advancing your savant domain. Think of the emotional highs in a productive savantflow, when you are achieving at your maximum and elements of your reality generated by the bioflow are helping you every step of the way.

Imagine getting the exact information you need when you need it to achieve a goal. Or a model that will show you how to get what you want. Or clusters of coincidences catapulting you ahead – each one a magical mystical experience. Imagine the emotional highs of breakthroughs and epiphanies creating unprecedented futures.

This is the stuff of a life of miracles. Awe will become a frequent feature of living the savanting modus operandi. Imagine looking back across major creations and inventions in your savant domain, especially if you've been a nonperformer before savanting. Then imagine that you achieved all of that through play not work. Imagine how the world would be different because you lived and left your footprint.

WHOLENESS FOR THE DAMAGED

One of the most frequently mentioned dimensions of
the flow experience is that, while it lasts, one is able
to forget all the unpleasant aspects of life.
Mihaly Csikszentmihalyi,
Flow: The Psychology of Happiness[71]

Respite and self-transcendence

Awe is a sought-after emotional goal for everyone, but it is heavenly for "the damaged." I want to encourage those who think themselves too damaged from abuse, trauma, or psychological or physical limitations to pursue self-actualization, self-transcendence, and worldchanging goals to switch to the savanting modus operandi.

There are no negative emotions experienced during savantflows. Imagine the hours, days, and years of relief that those tormented by looping negative thoughts or addictions might have. If you want an escape from the noise in your head holding you back, savanting creates a place where innate drives and biochemical rewards can pull you to do your greatest work.

As the beneficial addiction to advance one's savant domain takes hold, lives that might otherwise have been wasted through psychological issues and complications will be pulled to achieve great meaning and contribution.

Savanting may be a most unexpectedly profound psychological solution. It is a step beyond Viktor Frankl's logotherapy based on "our will to meaning." Savanting addresses "our will to meaning" and "our will to creativity, creation, invention, innovation," and "our need to contribute" as an integrated process.

Repair

But more than relief, serial savantflows may be able to correct the problems of the damaged so they can become whole. Savantflows provide some extremely positive emotional, spiritual, and even mystical experiences that are rejuvenating.

Damaged individuals may thrive in savantflows where their damage either doesn't exist or is not invoked. And, over months and years devoid of re-damaging cycles, the hold of old noise in one's head will dissipate. It will be overwritten by new more positive habits and thoughts.

In addition, activities triggering savantflows are often ones which creatively express, reinforce, and nourish one's essence. These often lead to experiencing self-sufficient, sustainable self-love – often the missing ingredient that resulted in the damage in the first place.

While there are no studies specifically investigating savantflows, there are flow studies which reinforce these findings. There was a 2009 study conducted on Japanese students by Kiyoshi Asakawa at the Department of Intercultural Communication at Hosei University Chiyoda-ku in Tokyo, Japan.

The study found that those who experienced flow more often were more likely to have higher levels of self-esteem, Jujitsu-kan (a sense of fulfillment), life satisfaction, better coping strategies, and lower anxiety.[72]

If you're in therapy to deal with your lack of fulfillment, even ordinary flows may be an alternate way to achieve this goal. As one's time in savantflows increases and significant projects start to define one's savant domain, positive emotions will emerge around self-love, self-esteem, self-respect, self-confidence, and a strengthened identity and purpose. Sustainable happiness is possible from accelerated and amplified achievement and the increased creativity of savantflows.

Those damaged by deprivation or interference with this critical suite of emotions can be made whole. This is just one more way in which human biology has been designed to be self-correcting. Evolution would of course have built a powerful constellation of positive and compelling emotions into Man's maximum to entice repeated reentry to savantflows?

The damaged may still reveal their flaws in other arenas of their lives. However, if they can concentrate their lives on activities which generate savantflow and integration with the bioflow, their damage will not be triggered. They'll be pulled towards forums for their art that invoke savantflows where negative emotions are replaced with emotional highs.

Addiction

If substance addictions are biology-based, then invoking the different biological pathways inherent in savanting may lessen or eliminate their pull. If substance abuse is a way to avoid emptiness, then the meaningful work in savantflows will offer an alternate route. Evolution has ensured that we have many drives and biochemical draws to keep us pursuing a savantflow way of life. Over time, they may become the substance of choice for addicts.

> *The only happy people I know are the ones who are working well at something they consider important.*
> Abraham Maslow

---

[68]   Keltner and Haidt (2003), "*Approaching awe, a moral, spiritual, and aesthetic emotion*," in *Cognition and Emotion*, 2003, 17 (2), 297-314

[69]   Keltner, D. J., & Haidt, J. (2003). Approaching awe, a moral, spiritual, and aesthetic emotion. *Cognition and Emotion*, *17*(2), 297–314. https://doi.org/10.1080/02699930302297

[70]   The nature of awe: Elicitors, appraisals, and effects on self-concept by Michelle N. Shiota and Dacher Keltner, University of California, Berkeley, CA, USA and Amanda Mossman, University of California, Santa Barbara, CA, USA, Psychology Press, Taylor & Francis Group, Cognition and Emotion 2007, 21 (5), 944-963. Also https://greatergood.berkeley.edu/dacherkeltner/docs/shiota.2007.pdf 4-6-1

[71]   Mihaly Csikszentmihalyi, *Flow: The Psychology of Happiness* 1992, Ebury Publishing, November 15, 2013

[72]   Kiyoshi Asakawa, *Flow Experience, Culture, and Well-being: How Do Autotelic Japanese College Students Feel, Behave, and Think in Their Daily Lives?*, Journal of Happiness Studies, April 2010, Volume 11, Issue 2, pp 205–223 |Department of Intercultural Communication, Hosei University Chiyoda-ku, Tokyo, Japan, Research Paper, First Online: 04 January 2009, K. J. Asakawa, Happiness Stud (2010) 11: 205. https://doi.org/10.1007/s10902-008-9132-3 http://www.springerlink.com/content/xl76g47386275241/ https://link.springer.com/journal/10902/11/2/page/1 https://link.springer.com/article/10.1007%2Fs10902-008-9132-3#citeas

24

Purpose

*Each person comes into this world with a specific
destiny – he has something to fulfill, some message
has to be delivered, some work has to be completed.
You are not here accidentally – you are here
meaningfully. There is a purpose behind you. The
whole intends to do something through you.*
Osho

So many have an emptiness that causes them to yearn for more
meaning, purpose, and mission in their lives. They feel
purpose is the key to a plethora of desirable psychological,
physical, material, and emotional rewards that they crave from their
core.

In fact, this need is so widespread that one could assume that
it is genetic. And it would be understandable why evolution might
select for such a yearning to pull us to protect, adapt, and advance
the species.

The methods currently popular for discovering one's purpose
are rather haphazard – yielding imperfect, incorrect, temporary,
burdensome, or unsustainable directions. Savanting more precisely
satisfies this craving for the desired emotional state of having
purpose.   Instead of having to rely on human intelligence to
determine one's purpose, savanting conscripts nature's intelligence.
Our purpose and even the need for a purpose are biology-driven.

SAVANTING'S BIOLOGY-DRIVEN PURPOSE

Biology is used in savanting not only to identify your purpose but also to drive it, evolve it, and adapt it throughout your life as you grow and as your context progresses. The bioflow tells you when you are on purpose and maximized within your savant domain by responding with support.

Biological mechanisms which have evolved over generations as part of our biological imperative determine what we now label "our purpose." It need not be the confusing intellectual exercise that so many seekers endure to find meaning in their lives.

In addition, most popular methods for defining one's purpose yield a goal-driven approach – a mission that you must achieve even if you dislike what you have to do to get there. Savanting instead provides a state-driven approach. It addresses the real goal – sustainably generating the fulfilling state of being that you are craving. This is the underlying driver of the careers of our six superachievers.

This state is achieved and sustained by doing the most meaningful, intrinsically rewarding activities at your biological maximum with continuity. Each of these activities build on each other throughout your lifetime until your legacy becomes significant worldchanging work. You *live* your purpose rather than *know* where it will lead. You have the "emotion of purpose" every day in savantflow as you scale frontier after frontier within your savant domain.

Savanting provides the means to sustain a state of peak-purpose, peak-meaning, peak-growth, peak-performance, peak-achievement, and peak-creation in the territory of your greatest talents and passion. It is the guidance system so many of us seek to keep us on-path throughout our lives.

Your ideal "purpose" then would be the same as your savant formula. It would have you operating at your biological maximum so that you can apply your strongest most rewarding talents to the most meaningful, intrinsically rewarding activities for an audience that will value this, your greatest work. Add to this formula the support of the bioflow to help you outperform your innate potential and you have the only logical foundation upon which to build your life's work.

Now that you know about the bioflow, do you really want to risk committing to a life purpose which requires you to fight continuously upstream against its direction? The advantage of savanting for identifying and implementing your purpose is that your pathway, at any point in your life, will be clear.

There will be clear signals inside and outside of you when you are moving in the right direction. The ideal path for your maximization can be determined at any point based on the empirical evidence of bioflow support in your past which will predict future bioflow support and hence your ideal direction. *You are guided.*

Even nonvisionaries can operate as if they have a vision of the future because they are guided by the evolutionary flow of humanity. Even the execution-challenged may operate with the genius of execution creatives such as the four founders of Amazon, Facebook, Microsoft, and Apple. Even noncreatives may generate the new and unprecedented.

You are supported. You have relevant information at the right time from the bioflow for a re-combining process which produce new information systems to advance your savant domain. You will enjoy coincidence after coincidence catapulting you ahead to a goal which may be better than the one you pursued when you started.

How helpful is it to have a guidance system which is up to date with all the new inventions, innovations, and events in your savant domain despite you not knowing about any of them? You will have a better chance of achieving your purpose when you go with the flow. One's savant formula provides a new more reliable way for determining one's purpose and living it.

DETERMINING YOUR BIOLOGY-DRIVEN PURPOSE

To launch your biology-driven purpose, you need only to begin doing activities or pursuing learning that you are passionate about which will put you into a savantflow. How do you know which activities are likely to invoke savantflows? There are two ways to predict these.

First, activities which provoked savantflows in your past will likely generate savantflows in your future. Savantflows will have the telltale signs of support from the bioflow. The savantflows will conform to a pattern or theme over time. Your life purpose and your savant domain will emerge from that order.

Savantflows are high-growth states. Your purpose is going to evolve with serial savantflows as you do. The "emotional feel of being on purpose" will provide you with better direction indicators than trying to apply labels to define and pursue your purpose.

Eventually, you'll be able to look back with 20:20 hindsight and see how your biological wiring in partnership with the bioflow has perfectly advanced you along a logical pathway that defines an identifiable purpose. Then you can project that purpose into the future to accelerate your progression.

The second way in which you can predictably determine which activities are likely to generate the savantflows defining your purpose is through other themes of activities supported by the bioflow in your past. You can identify the direction of your purpose from any of several interchangeable themes or patterns of events in your past because they are all leading you to the same place. Biological maximization.

Your unpaid work theme, your knowledge-pursuit theme, your creativity-pursuit theme, your frontier-pursuit theme, or the theme of activities that triggered relevant spontaneous knowledge, clusters of coincidences, or spontaneous creativity. Each one of these themes will identify your biology-driven purpose.

Just begin. Find safe places, projects, or activities to begin the process. The block and flow events in your reality will tell you whether you are going in the direction supported by the bioflow for your purpose. You'll have all the distinct telltale signs to confirm that you're moving along your purpose path. You'll be attracting people, events, and information into your life routinely which will feed and facilitate the advance of your purpose.

An intrinsically rewarding purpose

I want to reiterate a concept in the context of this discussion of biology-driven purpose. The activities that are part of your purpose will be intrinsically rewarding. This is not about doing activities you are excited about to achieve a particular goal. "Intrinsically rewarding" or "biologically rewarding" mean that the activity itself is the goal.

Think of our six superachievers. Their childhood play became their adult paid play in the savant domain in which they became famous. Their careers were biologically not intellectually driven. So many seekers never find their purpose because this singular requirement was never met. Instead of concentrating their time on intrinsically rewarding activities and letting a purpose-related context unfold, they instead sought a goal and took action – often unpleasant action – to achieve that goal.

Your lifework may lie in a field which does not yet exist. Or there may be a channel from which to launch it which never occurred to you. There may be coincidences which can save you hundreds of steps to accelerate your start. There may be a few models for how to proceed which, when you combine them together will lead to a worldchanging, paradigm-shifting breakthrough.

Begin with what you know to try to trigger engaging addictive, emotionally rewarding savantflows. What feels good; what you are passionate about; what is meaningful; what is fun; and so on. When you discover your purpose, it will rely on work that is its own reward. You cannot enter savantflow without this.

Accordingly, it is also important not to choose work that you *think* will get you to the intrinsically rewarding work or place that you want to be. This is contrary to the biological functioning and benefits of savanting. You'll have none of the magic working for you.

> ...[Flow] is when we act freely, for the sake of the
> action itself rather than for ulterior motives, that we
> learn to become more than what we were.
> Mihaly Csikszentmihalyi,
> Flow: The Psychology of Optimal Experience (1990)

OTHER VIEWS ON PURPOSE

A self-actualization purpose

To discover one's life purpose before savanting, I think many people gravitated towards Maslow's self-actualization concept – with or without his self-transcendence embellishment. Maslow's self-actualization is the need to become what one has the potential to be.

However, when it comes to implementation, Maslow's formula lack's the executable precision that savanting has for discovering your purpose within his self-actualization goal. As a result, Maslow's self-actualization goal has sent people on a frustrating path to the unattainable.

In addition, to some extent, Maslow is suggesting a goal state. Savanting instead offers a way of life that will have you operating sustainably in the self-actualization state around your purpose. Intellectually defined goals can take you off your state of biological maximization.

Is Nirvana our purpose?

Many seek as their purpose the aspirations of a multitude of religions and spiritual disciplines for nirvana, bliss, eternal peace, heaven on earth, nonduality, or a union with the God consciousness. From a biology perspective, enduring bliss or peace is unfortunately not sustainable.

Human biology is not designed to arrive at and sustain an emotional state such as bliss or love without continuous re-stimulation by differing stimuli. There is something called habituation which causes us to adapt to a series of identical stimuli – pain or pleasure.

Therefore, nonrepeating stimuli are always required to sustain any state – pain or pleasure – in the face of biomechanisms which promote habituation to identical stimuli. We need the constant replenishment of stimuli available through our everchanging peak-growth savantflows.

Here is how I viewed this in "Peak Evolution" in 2001: " . . . there can be no arrival at a blissful state and then the maintenance of that state by clinging to the stimuli or symbols that invoked it. This is a false dream that must be replaced by a more insightful understanding of the nature of the human being.

"As creative beings, we are designed to be perpetually creating. Continuous bliss comes from flowing with the dynamic creativity of the universe. Accept this and then master the process."[73] I realized early in my journey to develop savanting that we were biologically wired to be in a state of perpetual creativity in which we are continuously changing our world in some way.

So here is my reasoning for how to achieve a "Nirvana" purpose through savanting. In savantflows there are only positive emotions. Amabile's studies at Harvard demonstrate that creativity is increased in flow states and that it lasts for days after the flow event. In addition, self-transcendent flows orchestrated by the bioflow, such as we saw in the lives of our six superachievers, last considerably longer than regular flow states.

The emotion I see most often from people in savantflow is self-love. Think of someone talking ecstatically about what they have created or a singer expressing him or herself passionately in savantflow. The excitement and enthusiasm or passion are obvious. But as you empathize with them, you'll realize they are experiencing sustainable self-sufficient self-love. Happiness is inherent in self-love.

This is not nirvana in a religious sense. However, it might very well be a substitute life purpose for many. It is more quickly and more effectively achieved through savanting than any religious or spiritual disciplines. This is because the latter requires moral codes and unnatural practices to achieve this goal state and they tend to demand people step out of life rather than into it. Savanting is an action-based, living state which works *with* biology both internal and external to us.

"Man is originally characterized by his "search for meaning" rather than his "search for himself." The more he forgets himself – giving himself to a cause or another person – the more human he is. And the more he is immersed and absorbed in something or someone other than himself the more he really becomes himself."

Viktor E. Frankl, *Man's Search for Ultimate Meaning*

The will to power – pleasure – meaning – creativity

I made a case for our creative expression being our purpose in "Peak Evolution" (2001, 2010). I contrasted that viewpoint with some rather famous alternative purposes: "I've found creation and creativity so effective in optimizing, normalizing and transforming individuals that I now believe that 'the will to creativity' is the major motivational force in human beings.

"Sigmund Freud's psychoanalysis was based on the will to pleasure. Alfred Adler's psychology and Friedrich Nietzsche's philosophy promoted 'the will to power' and the foundation of psychologist Viktor Frankl's logotherapy is 'the will to meaning.' No matter which of these I tried to identify for a client, it always came back to the power or freedom to create.

"What was innately meaningful to a client turned out to be the creation of a new reality or just a creation in general. This is why I believe that 'the will to creation,' or 'the drives to creativity and creation,' are actually what motivates us.

"We crave to change the world with our meaningful creations. We seek to be part of something greater than ourselves. We seek to know ourselves by our creative expression. Creativity and creation are an underlying theme of 'Peak Evolution' since the naturality paradigm mirrors the same underlying theme in the universe."[74]

To my continuing belief in a creativity purpose after almost twenty years, let me add reinforcement from creativity expert Robert

Fritz, "There is a deep longing to create that resides within the soul of humanity. Beyond our natural instinct for survival. . . . we also have an instinct for building, organizing, forming, and creating."[75]

Robert Fritz is the founder of DMA® and Technologies for Creating®. With Charlie Keifer, Peter Senge, and Peter Stroh, hc also co-founded Innovation Associates, a company dedicated to helping to build organizations using principles of the creative process.

Fritz goes on to say "What motivates a creator? The desire for the creation to exist. A creator creates in order to bring the creation into being. People in the reactive-responsive orientation often have trouble understanding this sensibility: to create for the sake of the creation itself. Not for the praise, not for the 'return on investment,' not for what it may say about you, but for its own sake."[76]

Here, Fritz is reinforcing my advice to pursue intrinsically rewarding activities as an end in themselves. Julia Cameron states in "The Artist's Way" (1992) that "Creativity is the natural order of life. Life is energy: pure creative energy." Cameron's philosophy is that every person is born with the right and the ability to be "creative."

Religious leader and airline president Dieter F. Uchtdorf gave a moving talk to the General Relief Society Meeting in 2008 entitled "Happiness, Your Heritage." He said, "The desire to create is one of the deepest yearnings of the human soul. No matter our talents, education, backgrounds, or abilities, we each have an inherent wish to create something that did not exist before. . . . But to what end were we created? We were created with the express purpose and potential of experiencing a fulness of joy. Our birthright – and the purpose of our great voyage on this earth – is to seek and experience eternal happiness.   One of the ways we find this is by creating things."

Life is never made unbearable by circumstances, but
only by lack of meaning and purpose.
Viktor E. Frankl

---

[73]   Lauren Holmes, 2001/2010, *Peak Evolution: Beyond Peak Performance and Peak Experience*, Chapter 14, *Beyond Flow: Egolessness, Nonduality and Oneness*
[74]   Lauren Holmes, 2001/2010, *Peak Evolution*, Chapter 2, The Ten Optimizers, 5. Our Creativity Drives
[75]   Robert Fritz, *Creating*, 1981, Page 3 Ballantine Books; Reprint edition March 31 1993
[76]   Robert Fritz, *The Path of Least Resistance*, 1984, 1989, The Random House Publishing Group

25

Our Savant-Domain Creational Purpose

For the person with creative potential there is no
wholeness except in using it.
Robert K. Greenleaf, The Servant as Leader

The demand for creativity

For several years, "creativity" has been selected as one of the topmost required skills by the Partnership for 21st Century Skills – a collection of 250 researchers at 60 institutions.[77] Creativity has also been selected as the "most crucial factor for future success" in an IBM survey of 1500 chief executive officers in 60 countries. The IBM 2010 Global CEO Study[78] found that "chief executives believe successfully navigating an increasing complex world will require creativity."

Unfortunately, we still face the challenge for how to train people to be more creative. However, savanting is a method for increasing creativity, creations, innovations, and unprecedented solutions from even noncreatives.

There have not been any studies done on the savantflows which are the main dynamic underlying savanting. However, even the study of regular flow states validates savanting's claim to increase creativity.

Creating the Creative

Teresa Amabile is the Edsel Bryant Ford Professor of Business Administration and a Director of Research at Harvard Business School. Amabile's studies show that people are more creative in flow and, surprisingly, also the day or days following a flow state.

This suggests that flow doesn't just heighten creativity in the moment. It heightens it long-term. In other words, Amabile's work demonstrates that being in flow trains (or re-trains) people to be more creative.[79] Her findings are reinforced by the top flow expert himself, Mihaly Csikszentmihalyi, in his book "Creativity: The Psychology of Discovery and Invention."[80]

With the coordinated neurochemical, neuroelectrical, and neuroanatomical changes in brain function experienced during flow, we have an exceptionally potent workaround for the challenge of teaching people how to be more creative.

Rather than addressing this challenge directly, we may instead address the much easier challenge of developing people's ability to enter flow. The neurobiology inherent in flow states will then trigger the increase in creativity.

Because savanting is based on serial savantflows, it dramatically increases creativity not only because of the flow brain but also because of the savant-like information inflow. Savant brains and savantflow brains seem to have surprisingly similar externally sourced savant genius.

The difference is that, in nonsavants, information inflow relevant to the current flow-state activity is presented to a flow brain primed for breakthroughs, epiphanies, and flashes of genius. It is therefore not necessary to have well developed creative skills.

Instead you can apply logic to combine the exact pieces of information you need for a creative solution. In fact, this logic component may be the real explanation as to why creativity has proven to be a whole-brain activity and not simply a right-brain activity as previously thought.

Born Creative

We have been accumulating throughout the book several proofs that we are creative beings and that our purpose is creative self-expression. The breadth and depth of generations of biological adaptations that enhance human ability to create and promote our addiction to it are quite striking. The drives, the emotional highs, the peak-performance and peak-growth highs, the gratifying biochemistry, the addictive qualities of creativity and of the flow states that enhance creativity are a few examples.

The evolutionary machinery obviously favored our species having the creativity necessary to adapt and advance for improved survivability. Perhaps the strongest proof that we are creative beings is that the NASA study conducted by Dr. George Land demonstrated that we are born creative and lose it with our entry into the school system.[81]

Evidence of our creational purpose

I have speculated about how and why savants have access to the massive information that is behind the superskills in their savant domain. Given evolution's goals, I assume that we evolved the capability for the information inflow we observe in savants in order to fuel the creativity behind our adaptivity.

Evolution seems to have consistently subscribed to the idea that the more creative and adaptive we are, the more likely our species will survive and thrive. A multitude of mutations and mechanisms demonstrate this. This is why I've come to hypothesize that our shared purpose is creational. This is what one would expect if we were creative beings.

If my hypothesis is correct about evolution having cultivated human ability to access savant-like information inflow in order to fuel the creative process, we could reasonably assume that, despite their damaged brains, some savants would be able to complete the second part of the creative process – the re-combining of their information fuel to generate new creations.

This indeed is the case. Over time, some savant brains grow to make the connections necessary to use that information fuel for creativity and creations. Human creativity therefore does seem to be evolution's goal.

Savant creativity

I've presented my case already for my hypothesis that the information necessary to savant genius is externally sourced. I've presented my logic behind a hypothesis that we are creative beings with a biology-driven purpose of creative self-expression. Now I'm examining my hypothesis that the purpose for the massive information inflow behind savant superskills is for the first part of the creative process. The fuel.

For this to be true, some savants would have to be able to complete the second part of the creative process – that of re-combining this information fuel to yield novel creations in their savant domain. This is the case.

The latest savant research shows that over time the damaged brains of savants have sufficient plasticity to adapt so they are able to create. Many scientists now suspect that all human brains have this same degree of plasticity.

There is this mythology that says that when people
are born, their brains are essentially fixed very early
on and they're not able to change their connections.
I was aware that was a myth and that people could
learn new skills.
Daniel Tammet, a high-functioning autistic savant

Therefore, we may all become more creative at any point in our lives just as some savants have done. In fact, the challenge identified in the *Creating the Creative* section above may instead be one of re-releasing our innate creativity. In theory, we should all be able to return to the 98% creativity that the NASA study by Dr. George Land showed for children under five.

So let's look at the evidence to prove my hypothesis – if humans are meant to be creative beings in their savant domains, we would expect some savants to be able to complete that creativity cycle.

Savant expert, Dr. Darold A. Treffert initially thought savants were not capable of creativity in his original 1988 version of "Extraordinary People: Understanding Savant Syndrome." However, with additional years of observation with the same patients, Treffert noticed a "predictable and replicable sequence of steps that progresses from imitation, to improvisation, to creation in savant syndrome."[82]

In his article, "Savant Syndrome 2013 – Myths and Realities," Treffert references examples of savants moving through this progression. For example, within 10 years, the blind American savant Leslie Lemke progressed from flawless music replication to improvising in ecstatic states reminiscent of savantflow experiences. Several years later Lemke began composing his own music which became progressively more unique over time.

British savant Stephen Wiltshire – identified earlier as "the human camera" – drew a highly accurate map of the London skyline from memory after a single helicopter trip over the city. However, Treffert also saw a progression in Stephen from replication to improvisation to free-form creation.

High-functioning autistic savant Daniel Tammet has written best-selling books and even created his own language. He is helping us to understand how savants operate and, with his "uncalculated" mathematical calculations, reinforced my hypothesis for externally sourced savant genius.

> *I am unusually creative—from visualizing numerical landscapes composed of random strings of digits to the invention of my own words and concepts in numerous languages.*
> Daniel Tammet, a high-functioning autistic savant

Treffert also references Matt Savage who advanced from playback to jazz improvisation to the creation of his own jazz pieces. Another musical savant, Hikari Oe, grew to prefer composing to performing – a rare reversal of the bias of most musical savants.

Dr. Treffert concludes, "So the savant can be creative. Some savants prefer to stay with replication, but many have gone beyond literal copying, as stunning as that can be, to improvisation and then creation of something entirely new."[83]

This finding of creativity in savants supports my hypothesis that the information inflow we are trying to duplicate to achieve our own savant-like genius, may indeed be part of the internal-external machinery our species has evolved. Our cultures have simply interfered with our innate information-access mechanisms necessary to fuel the creativity behind the adaptivity that will bolster our chances for surviving and thriving.

Land's study shows this occurring at age five, right when I have hypothesized our culturally pressured disconnection from the bioflow in order to become beings who end at our skin. Our six superachievers show what is possible if that disconnect never occurs or if one can restore the link through savanting.

Accessing savant-domain information fuel

There is more confirmation of my hypothesis of our creational purpose and it just happens to reinforce my first hypothesis of externally sourced savant genius. I have speculated that savant brains and savantflow brains operating similarly. They are both in activity fusion within flow state when information inflow occurs. Both brains are focused on a single activity in the individual's savant domain.

This seems to be the formula for accessing precisely the information relevant to the activity which triggered the current savantflow. The more information systems relevant to the task at hand that you have available, the more likely it is that you can re-combine them to generate novel systems or original creations. This would explain the increase in creativity in regular flow states witnessed by Teresa Amabile's studies at Harvard.

The altered states of awareness or consciousness documented by Csikszentmihalyi for flow states then are not random. They are part of this information inflow system and the creational re-combining process as well. Each expansion of consciousness or breadth of view enables us to "see" more information, more interconnections among information systems, more dynamics as to where relevant systems are advancing, more trends, more patterns, and so on.

Our various awarenesses in savantflow are part of a consciousness continuum based on an ever-widening aperture revealing more information or allowing greater information inflow.

The widening of the aperture diameter is what enables spontaneous knowledge events identified for savanting –

breakthroughs, epiphanies, flashes of genius, and enlightenment events.

The difference between a breakthrough and the all-knowingness of a spiritual or ecstatic event then is simply one of degree. A change in the diameter of the aperture. Opening the aperture fully will trigger nondual, unity or cosmic consciousness. These events are on the same continuum or part of the same information access capabilities observed for savants.

Unity consciousness is simply spontaneous knowledge events in which one's consciousness aperture is opened fully. To experience unity consciousness then one simply needs to increase time in savantflows. This is the source of my own ability to routinely access this breadth of perspective – a skill I did not possess until I began pursuing my savant domain through serial savantflows of ever-increasing depth.

I have referenced the download of "personbooks," "factbooks," and "procedurebooks" since Chapter 6, *Savant-Like Information Access by NonSavants*. These are examples of exactly the same aperture phenomenon. You can perhaps now see more clearly how it could indeed be a possibility to download your own "personbook" to achieve enlightenment as Lao Tzu suggests.

Or you can download one "book" containing everything by opening your aperture 100% to spontaneously experience cosmic consciousness. In the flash of a fully expanded aperture, you could glimpse how the universe works and how to harness it to achieve your life goals just as those who've had a near death experience do. You could instantly know your purpose for being here, your highest level of contribution, and the only work you should consider doing.

I suspect that in all moments of enlightenment ever experienced, the individual was learning or creating in savantflow within their savant domain. These types of experiences are not ends in and of themselves. They are part of our information access apparatus to fuel the creations which will give us "the emotional state of purpose" we are all biologically biased to seek.

Our savant-domain creational purpose

For those seeking to define their purpose, I believe we can now further refine that process. I am obviously strongly committed to the *biology-driven purpose* defined through savanting. Our six superachievers reinforce that concept. However, I believe this identification of one's purpose may be further narrowed from a creational focus in general to savant-domain creativity in particular.

The purpose of each and every one of us then is intrinsically rewarding learning and creational activities in savantflows which are the creative expression of our biological essence. In other words, we may now narrow our purpose, first, to a creational purpose – we are meant to be creative beings – and finally to our ultimate purpose – our savant-domain creativity – creations which advance our savant domains through frontier after frontier.

Renowned American cognitive psychologist Howard Gardner was right in 1993 when he determined that our creativity is confined to the domain of our greatest strength. Everyone now has the means to more precisely determine and then sustainably pursue their true purpose.

Savanting provides a way to discover your life purpose with biological accuracy. It offers a way to dramatically increase the quantity and quality of your creations or creative impact on the world. It is the means to outperform your known potential.

Savanting is a new way to achieve mankind's most sought-after goals: self-actualization; self-transcendence; extreme self-knowledge; self-esteem; self-love; sustained happiness; respite, repair, and wholeness for the damaged; awe; expanded, unified and cosmic consciousness; and now purpose and meaning. It offers a new means for attaining peak performance, peak growth, peak creativity and operating at your true internal-external potential. Replicating externally sourced savant genius is now possible.

Savanting offers an alternative modus operandi – an alternative achievement protocol – which may better explain the success of our six superachievers in a way that is replicable.

Bill Gates, Steve Jobs, Jeff Bezos, Mark Zuckerberg, Oprah, and Jim Carrey show us what could be accomplished after decades of accelerated growth and achievement at one's biological maximum in one's savant domain.

What will your equivalent to Microsoft, Gates Foundation, Apple, Pixar, Amazon, Blue Origin, Facebook, OWN Network, or "Eternal Sunshine of the Spotless Mind" look like?

There is one mind common to all individual men.
Every man is an inlet to the same and to all of the
same. He that is once admitted to the right of reason
is made a freeman of the whole estate. What Plato
has thought, he may think; what a saint has felt, he
may feel; what at any time has befallen any man, he
can understand. Who hath access to this universal
mind is a party to all that is or can be done, for this is
the only and sovereign agent.
Ralph Waldo Emerson, Essays: First Series 1

All power is of one kind, a sharing of the nature of
the world. The mind that is parallel with the laws of
nature will be in the current of events, and strong
with their strength.
Emerson, Power, *The Conduct of Life*

[77]   Steven Kotler, *Flow States and Creativity: Can you train people to be more creative?* Psychology Today, Feb 25, 2014
https://www.psychologytoday.com/ca/blog/the-playing-field/201402/flow-states-and-creativity?amp

[78]   *IBM 2010 Global CEO Study: Creativity Selected as Most Crucial Factor for Future Success*, News Release, Armonk, NY, 18 May 2010. https://www-03.ibm.com/press/us/en/pressrelease/31670.wss

[79]   Steven Kotler, *The Playing Field, Psychology Today, Flow States and Creativity: Can you train people to be more creative?* Feb 25, 2014
https://www.psychologytoday.com/ca/blog/the-playing-field/201402/flow-states-and-creativity?amp

[80]   Mihaly Csikszentmihalyi, Creativity: The Psychology of Discovery and Invention, 2013, HarperCollins Publishers Ltd

[81]   Nick Skillicorn, *Evidence that children become less creative over time (and how to fix it),* August 5th, 2016 Chief Editor, Founder & CEO at Improvises Innovation Consulting,

[82]   Darold A. Treffert, MD, *Savant Syndrome 2013 — Myths and Realities* Wisconsin Medical Society
https://www.wisconsinmedicalsociety.org/professional/savant-syndrome/resources/articles/savant-syndrome-2013-myths-and-realities/

[83]   Darold A. Treffert, MD, *Savant Syndrome 2013 — Myths and Realities*

THE ENCORE

APPENDIX I: An Overview of Savanting

Excerpt from *The Encore: A Transformational Thriller*, from Chapter 3, *Connor's Council Speech* by Lauren Holmes (2018)

APPENDIX II: One's Savant Formula

Excerpt from *The Encore: A Transformational Thriller* from Chapter 11, *Heroes in the Making* by Lauren Holmes (2018)

BIOMAXED

APPENDIX III: Reset to your Maximum

Excerpt from BioMaxed: Chapters 30 and 31, *Reset to your Maximum* by Lauren Holmes (2019)

APPENDIX I: An Overview of Savanting

Excerpt from *The Encore: A Transformational Thriller*, **from Chapter 3,** *Connor's Council Speech* **by Lauren Holmes (2018)**

Connor stood at the head of the table collecting his thoughts on what he wanted to say. Suddenly his thoughts were arrested by the sheer beauty of the high-gloss, deeply burled wood of the long thick tabletop. He had never seen anything like it on Earth. The three-dimensional complexity and convolutions of the pronounced grain patterns pulled him into their depths, grounding him.

It incited within him a resonance upon which he had come to rely to signal that he was taking the right path. In an instant, everything he was about to say was recolored with new meaning and purpose. It was infused with new energy and inspiration. He was transformed from coerced to committed. He began his speech from a new depth.

"The simultaneous occurrence of a number of crises which threatened the survival of Earth and humanity fueled a dramatic change in the power structure which had dominated our planet. Those with the greatest power and/or money came to realize that all the power and money in the world were not going to save them. They had no choice but to relinquish the reins to 'lesser beings' more creative and talented than they were who could solve the problems.

"The creativity and inventiveness of the world's human resources were unleashed to find solutions. Brilliant breakthroughs defeated the crises. Humanity survived. Civilization evolved into a more advanced level of existence.

"I'd been recruited as Commander-in-Chief, Global Human Resources Maximization because I'd had unusual success over a few decades in creating worldchangers. Worldbuilders, may be more precise. The key to my methods was a dedication to the daily use and improvement of one's strongest most rewarding talents. This was our maximum. Our peak performance.

"I discovered that, once engaged, we had evolved mechanisms to addict us to operating at this maximum as you would expect of any successful species. My formula triggered these addictive survival mechanisms for maximization. Magic happened as a result of living this maximum day after day.

"An overdrive state emerged which exceeded known human potential. It was a state of genius which we routinely observe in savants who do not have the brain capacity to express such genius. It was the state of spontaneous knowledge which those who've had near death events universally describe.

"What emerged from my formula was serial breakthroughs, flashes of genius, creative inspirations, and other forms of spontaneous knowledge. Whole systems or 'books' of relevant information seem to download into their heads to help them complete the task at hand. One breakthrough could bypass hundreds of steps necessary to achieving a goal.

"The internal mechanisms humans had evolved to pressure peak performance to improve our chances of survival include addictive drives, biochemistry, positive emotions and passions, to name a few.

"These mechanisms are part of the same system we have evolved to maximize the health of our bodies. But our pressure to maximize appears to be larger than an internal maximizing process.

"It became evident that human beings are linked to a larger external maximization process with which they have co-evolved. This external maximizing machinery seeks to maximize all living things synergistically, symbiotically, and synchronously.

"This extension of our internal resources with external resources was the source of the overdrive state I discovered. It was a new level of peak performance and human potential. The formula I invented was the means to invoke this overdrive state.

"Recruiting this external maximization machinery occurs automatically when one is operating at one's maximum. This is because maximization internally and externally is a single system. We have not evolved to operate as separate entities. When one is complying with the direction of one's maximizing machinery internally, one will automatically merge with the external maximizing machinery.

"Because this machinery is advancing all living systems, I call it *the bioflow*. It is the direction of the co-evolution of all living species. When we comply with the bioflow, our capabilities are suddenly extended by the power, information, direction, synergy, and evolution of all living systems. We can achieve beyond our internal potential.

"To complete my overdrive formula, I discovered a fast route to maximization. A built-in mechanism that humanity has evolved. I discovered *savantflow*. We've all experienced ordinary flow states. They are periods of altered consciousness that arise from hyperfocus on an activity.

"They are sessions of complete absorption in an activity such that time, place, and sense of self disappear. They invoke activity fusion, if you will. Normally, our brains fire chaotically. However, in flow, one's entire brain unifies to a cohesive focus on the activity at hand. Peak performance results."

"Are you talking about that 1990 book called *Flow: The Psychology of Optimal Experience* by a name I can't pronounce?" asked Nyhus as he looked up from his tablet.

"Csikszentmihalyi (cheek-sent-me-high-ee)," responded Connor. "And yes, this is the generic peak performance flow state to which I'm referring.

"Savantflow is a specialized subset which I identified. It occurs when the flow state experienced arises specifically from applying one's strongest most rewarding talents and strengths in the most meaningful way for the most appreciative or valuing audience.

"This is the formula for the true maximum performance of anyone's system. Savantflow is the way for us to automatically flick into maximized state."

Grand General Haugstad, the head of armed forces, interjected, "Did physicist David Bohm not talk about a 'holomovement.' How does this fit with the bioflow you're describing?"

"For simplicity, you can assume they are one and the same, Grand General Haugstad. You can assume a singular integrated, synergistic, and synchronous flow or pulsation for all successful living systems. Every successful living system is co-evolving dynamically." Haugstad nodded.

"This organizing bioflow continuously puts each living system into proximity with the information they need to advance and maximize," continued Connor. "Think of every living system as simply an information system.

"Think of nature as a librarian who organizes these living information systems to the advantage of the majority and priority. When one merges with the larger maximization machinery, the librarian will position you advantageously in the database to source the information you need next for the task you're focused on in your savantflow. The information you need for your continued or sustained maximization."

"You said 'goals which will maximize them,'" interrupted KahlDahr Chief of State Lennart Lorenson. "So then not every goal will be supported by the bioflow?"

"Correct, Minister Lorenson. And an astute observation. One must frame one's goal in the direction of the internal-external maximizing process if one wants the bioflow to accelerate and enhance its achievement. *Each of us can know what future goals will be supported based on what goals were supported in our past.*

"One's maximum is a constant. The way the bioflow pressures your system to maximize is a constant. Therefore, what was supported in your past will be supported in your future. You will know which projects will succeed or fail based on your history. *You'll have predictability.*

"If you're trying to obtain money to perpetuate a state of sub-maximization, or worse, a detrimental state, you'll have to fight upstream against a bioflow intent on maximizing you," explained Connor.

"Would the corollary be supported?" asked Rikard Riis. Connor had to smile to himself at Riis' interest in money. He'd already suspected that Riis was a puppet who could be bought.

"It's not as straightforward as that, Supreme Commander. Money for something on one's maximization path would be provided only if it is the fastest and easiest route to your maximization.

"We think we need money for every goal we want. Nature, however, is infinitely more creative. For example, one information coincidence might catapult you past hundreds of steps to your goal without the need for money. Accordingly, you'll want to be open to being orchestrated by the bioflow to achieving your goal through any channel rather than insisting it come through a specific channel such as money.

"*The goal of the internal-external maximizing machinery is to keep you in savantflow, your maximum state. Period.* You'll have to build your money goal in the direction that the bioflow is heading in order to benefit from it.

"I've already identified each living being as an information system," continued Connor. "Now I want you to think of creativity in information terms as well. *Creativity, creation, innovation, inventiveness, and creative breakthroughs are the result of combining existing information systems to create a new novel information system.*

"Think of the merging of a system of DNA information from each parent to create a new novel information system, a child. This recombining of information systems is how breakthroughs and epiphanies occur.

"This means that one will need easy access to the right information fuel to generate the breakthroughs necessary to solve Annutia's crises quickly. If you'll allow the bioflow to orchestrate your direction, you'll find yourself colliding with the exact information you need at the time you need it to re-combine for creative breakthroughs, flashes of genius, and Eureka events. This happens automatically with savantflow-bioflow integration.

"Over time, the magnitude, speed, quantity, quality, and impact of your breakthroughs will increase. Again, one breakthrough could eliminate hundreds of steps to achieve needed solutions faster. One breakthrough can change the world. One breakthrough can save a world in crisis. This means that even the ordinary can achieve the extraordinary.

"Obviously, the access to information fuel is key to the kind of serial breakthroughs we need to address Annutia's crises. Let me explain how I discovered how to increase the fuel to increase the breakthroughs.

"Mysteriously, savants usually display genius in one of five general fields — music, art, calendar recall or computation, mathematics, or mechanical/visual-spatial skills. A *music savant* may be able to perform an entire piece of music flawlessly after hearing it only once. Or, they may be able to play an instrument perfectly with no instruction or practice. Or, they may be able to demonstrate having an extensive repertoire of songs or pieces many of which they may never have heard before.

"*Calendar savants* can quickly identify the day of the week, the weather, and events for any calendar date past or present. *Mathematical savants* may be able to do rapid, complex calculations and equations in their heads in seconds. They can suddenly know the right mathematical answer even though most have brains incapable of even simple arithmetic.

"It gradually became obvious to me that most savants share a common skill – access to massive amounts of field-specific information which include procedural instructions. Savant superskills are information-based. Information and savantism are intimately linked. In some cases, the information base is itself the savant superskill as in *mnemonist savants*. Mnemonists have the ability to provide long lists of data such as names, numbers, entries in books, and so on."

"Do you mean a savant like Dustin Hoffman played in the movie *Rain Man*?" asked Axl.

"Precisely, Minister Plenipotentiary." Connor was delighted to discover another movie lover and another commonality with Axl. "Though fictional, he's the most famous savant. He's a composite of a few true savants.

"Through Raymond Babbitt, many of us were introduced to savants and learned what the human mind is capable of doing. You could see how Raymond was dysfunctional for so many things, but for capabilities based on access to a large database of information, he was a genius."

"Well, he must have been smart in some way to do the mathematical calculations he did," conjectured Rikard Riis.

"Or did he simply access calculations already in existence in a database of all potential calculations, Supreme Commander?" speculated Connor. His brain was too damaged to do the calculations or to retain the massive amounts of information which he demonstrated.

"I puzzled over why so many savants had precisely the same capabilities despite the variations in the damage to their left brains. Why did they access the same five or so databases of information? And why did those who acquired savantism later in life due to left-brain injury, suddenly know the same information about one of the savant field as other savants when they didn't know it before their injury?

"And why did so many savants access this information even though neuroscientists were able to prove that, like Raymond Babbitt, their brains should not be able to retain such information even if they could acquire it? This was all too coincidental to be simply an individual capability.   Something larger and more universal was going on.

"It suddenly occurred to me that every savant was downloading a single book or system of information from an external library specific to the field of their genius or talent. Suddenly, everything fit. Savants in each of the five fields of genius were downloading precisely the same book. If the book didn't exist how could they all have access to that same book? The information had to be externally sourced. This is why I now call my overdrive achievement methodology *savanting*.

"In savantflow, we automatically connect to the information database relevant to the activity which has generated the flow state. Therefore, we have many more breakthroughs when we're in savantflow. We have access to more information fuel relevant to our task at hand which can be re-combined to generate breakthroughs."

Azurite Chief of State Einar Nyhus looked up from researching on his tablet.   "Savant genius could indeed be externally sourced.   There is nothing in the Annutia or Earth databases which demonstrates that scientists have discovered mechanisms internal to savant brains which proves how their genius occurs.

"In fact, the study of savant brains has demonstrated the opposite – that savants should not be able to do the amazing things that they do. Commander Kane's explanation may indeed be the more plausible one."

"Thank you, Minister Nyhus. Creativity from non-creatives becomes possible with this new modus operandi," continued Kane.

"As with savants, the quantity and quality of the breakthroughs is not limited by one's intelligence, experience, or creativity.

"Rather it has to do with the access to information that results from integrating into the bioflow of nature's larger maximizing process. This automatically occurs in savantflow which is built into everyone. It is everyone's maximum state. Therefore, we could recruit an army of both creatives and non-creatives alike to help solve the Annutia crises.

"In addition, integration into the bioflow enables one's creativity to be guided in the direction of humanity's evolutionary flow. This means that the breakthroughs one will have will be important to the evolving human race. This integration is why a Bill Gates, Steve Jobs, or Jeff Bezos could invent at the front end of the evolution of civilization thus ensuring their products and services would be popular. They lived in savantflow.

"Therefore, connecting to the bioflow is how we'll ensure that we'll have the specific breakthroughs necessary to save Annutia. The bioflow is already trying to correct the damaged living systems of the planet. If we tap into that, our efforts will be synergistic with nature's efforts.

"To enter flow or savantflow, one must be stretched beyond one's previous capabilities. Consequently, growth is built in. The more time you spend in savantflow, the faster your functionality and strengths will increase. Therefore, over time, your system's maximum will increase.

"Because flow is an altered state of consciousness, one's consciousness will also develop over time. Specifically, serial savantflow sessions will cause your consciousness or breadth of perspective to expand.

"What does this mean for you? If you're sitting in a rowboat on a river, your view of the events in your life might be like seeing boxes float past you. However, if you're in a hot air balloon above the river, you might see a pattern in those boxes or that they're connected into a system. From a plane you might be able to see that that system of boxes was connected to four other systems upon which you might capitalize to meet your goals.

"Eventually continuous expansion will lead each individual to experience unity consciousness. This means you can see and capitalize on the interconnectedness of all things for each territory upon which you choose to focus.

The solutions you can contribute to the world from this state will increase exponentially. With unity consciousness and immersion into the bioflow, you'll have more information upon which to make decisions. You'll also have more information to combine into new information systems.

"In addition, expanded consciousness will also trigger a cascading increase in your baseline functionality. Especially your meta-competencies. Cognitive skills, for example, will improve. There'll be upgrades in abstract thinking, conceptual thinking, big-picture thinking, systems thinking, strategic thinking, mental agility, adaptivity, pattern recognition, trend perception, environmental scanning, problem re-framing, and ambiguity resolution.

"Now imagine this kind of accelerated growth across Annutia's entire pool of human resources. You'll have raised the bar on the potential, the quality of life, and the operation of your entire civilization. You'll have made everyone's life more meaningful and contributory. You'll have linked everyone to the bioflow guidance system, so they're being orchestrated to the advantage of humanity."

"At this point, a global transformation will occur," continued Connor. He felt his frequency rising and those in the room coming with him as he continued to reveal compelling logic while bringing them to an emotional home innate in everyone.

"What will have emerged is a singular creative, inventive force directed by nature's evolutionary flow. The need for government control and direction will dissipate into distributed power and leadership. With every human being maximized in savantflow and moving with the bioflow, you'll have created unified direction and unified consciousness. You'll have a civilization based upon a single shared consciousness and purpose.

"Flow is an egoless state in which all that exists is the activity at hand. It is characterized by only positive emotions. Identity and separation cease to exist. Discrimination and conflict can therefore no longer exist. War will disappear. The fractionalization and segmentation of your society will fall away in this nature-run, talent-maximized world.

"Your society will have achieved spontaneous unification. All will become one. A single synergistic and synchronized oneness will emerge for the advance of humanity. *Universal peace and love would now be achievable as a byproduct of individual self-actualization and fulfillment.*"

APPENDIX II: One's Savant Formula

Excerpt from *The Encore: A Transformational Thriller* from Chapter 11, *Heroes in the Making* by Lauren Holmes (2018)

Connor addressed the class. "Good morning, everyone!" Audience members responded in kind. "Over the last few days, you've all been working hard to assimilate a new modus operandi for breakthroughs and creativity that we want you to use to solve the planet's crises.

"School is ending. Our time to begin implementation is at hand. We need to finalize a savant formula for each of you and identify the projects to which you will apply it. Think carefully about your selections as we step through a final review this morning. Let's begin.

"What is a savant formula?"

Sibylla Lund called out, "It's your maximum operation around the application of your strongest most rewarding talents. Your own maximization allows you to merge with the bioflow's maximization process. This enables your capabilities to be extended by those of the bioflow – its evolutionary direction, forces, information, and the capabilities of the living systems it orchestrates. This gives you the means to operate beyond your internal potential."

Sibylla was an unemployed electrical engineer from the shutdown of power plants due to the xenoforming and the switch to fossil fuels. She was referred to his Breakthru Mission by Axl Dahl's wife, Freya. She's a Varunian Freya met through her charity work.

"What else does bioflow integration give you, Sibylla?"

"It's also the means to access spontaneous knowledge as coincidences externally or as breakthroughs and epiphanies internally," continued Sibylla. "The more information fuel you have, the more easily, quickly, and frequently you can re-combine existing information systems to create a novel system or breakthrough that will get you to your goal more quickly.

"One breakthrough could bypass hundreds of steps requisite to achieving a goal. Our goal is to have serial breakthroughs driving our projects. Speed plus invention breakthroughs are of the essence. They are the key thrust of this Breakthru Mission since the normal modi operandi have failed to yield the necessary solutions to our crises. We're a world weak in creativity."

"Sibylla, I like how you've synthesized multiple lectures in a very net way," Connor responded, obviously impressed. "Well done.

"Why did I name your bioflow integration prescription your 'savant formula' and the new modus operandi 'savanting?'"

"It's the best explanation for how savants with no working left brains and thus no ability to access, retain, and process large quantities of data, nevertheless demonstrate that ability," explained Sibylla. "Their access must be external from information databases underlying the bioflow and all of its living information systems including the human species." Connor nodded.

"What is the generic formula for immersing oneself into the bioflow, Dania? Dania Lind suddenly became a deer in headlights. He hadn't meant to catch her off-guard. She had a Ph.D. in astrobiology after all and Sibylla had already given the high-level answer.

Oh. Connor suddenly realized that she was sitting next to Mikael Matsen again, the microbiologist. There was a romance forming between them, so she'd undoubtedly not heard his question.

"Anyone?" asked Connor as he tried to quickly take the spotlight off Dania. "What is the generic formula for immersing oneself into the bioflow?"

Gregor Stinar stood up. He was a lucky find assessed Connor. He'd just graduated top of his class with a master's degree in bioscience engineering and was an expert in environmental technology, rare for his and Annalise's tribe, the Azurites. Gregor had planned to take a year off to travel before settling into a career job. I suspect we wouldn't have acquired him otherwise Connor speculated.

Connor had had to ask Axl to get Azurite Chief of State Einar Nyhus to wine and dine Gregor to impress upon him that his planet needed him. Connor had heard something about a promise of first-class global travel that apparently sealed the deal.

"In its simplest form," began Gregor, "the bioflow is a machinery or set of mechanisms for maximizing living systems for survival. It promotes synergy among living systems. It orchestrates all living systems synchronously into the ideal evolutionary direction for all. Therefore, to integrate into it, one must be moving in the same direction or complying with its goals. One must be operating at one's maximum. Or at least doing activities which will eventually maximize you," Gregor added as an afterthought.

"Maximizing inside means you'll relink with the maximizing machinery outside since they are a single system. When you're complying with the direction and intent of the bioflow, you're letting nature maneuver you into your most advantageous position vis-à-vis other living systems, information, and resources."

"Extremely comprehensive answer, Greg. You're seeing the big picture – how all of the pieces fit together. You're understanding nature's goals and how to exploit them to accelerate your own goals. Thank you for an excellent overview.

"Greg tells us we need to be compliant with our internal maximizing mechanisms to merge with the external maximizing machinery. What then is our maximum?

Dania decided to respond. Connor was pleased that her head was back in the game. She was extremely talented and well-educated. Connor expected great things from her. He wanted to ensure she didn't waste her talents and opportunity for greatness on the distractions of a romance.

"Savantflow. And, before you ask," laughed Dania, "that's the flow state that arises when we're applying our strongest most rewarding talents to the most meaningful and gratifying tasks for an audience that values that work. The biochemistry and electromagnetics of our most desirable emotions, the constellation of our drives for achievement and creation, our maximization instincts and genes have all evolved to pull us to this maximum to ensure the survival of the individual and the species. Savantflow is our automatic mechanism for flicking us into our maximum."

"A very complete answer, Dania. Thank you. So how does one get into savantflow within the bioflow, Dania?"

"This is because your maximum is a constant and how the bioflow maximizes your system and indeed all living systems is also a constant. Suddenly you can seem to operate as if you have psychic abilities because you know which projects the bioflow will and will not support. Which projects will and will not succeed. Yet it's simply a matter of knowing nature's historical logic, goals, and directions."

"Yes, thank you, Dania," exclaimed Connor enthusiastically. He nodded at her with a proud grin to tell her that she had redeemed herself. "How does one discover one's savant formula?"

Olivia Ohlson stood up. She and Kellin's son Rolland were the youngest of the creatives at age 20. "To identify one's savant formula, we simply need to look at our past pattern of events and activities that launched our savantflows.

"Whatever the theme of the activities causing our savantflows was in the past – our *savantflows theme* – will predict how you can move into savantflow in the future. Your *savantflows theme* will be your *savant formula* for moving into future savantflows.

"Or, uh, I guess you could call it your *savantflow-bioflow theme*. It's this theme which will tell each of us precisely which projects to choose for success with Annutia's Breakthru Mission.

"Right you are, Olivia," confirmed Connor to validate both to Liv and the group that he respected how talented she was. She was another KahlDahr like Kellin and Rolland who was brilliant and inventive despite having been deprived of a formal education.

"*Savantflow-bioflow theme* captures our goal perfectly, doesn't it? Thank you, Olivia." Connor was pleased that he'd been right about Liv. Despite being so young she was excelling at savanting.

He had recruited her from the Programming Department after recruiting Kellin. Like Kellin, Liv had been overlooked as all KahlDahr are. Their protruding brows make them appear both menacing and primitive. Also, she was female, beautiful, poor, confident, creative, and self-educated, all of which increased the discrimination she had endured over her short life.

The ruling castes had missed that, with Liv's unity consciousness, she could see how massive computer systems fit together. She had an executive perspective. Yet she could also work brilliantly on all the tiny details composing that larger picture.

He and Annalise had been waiting for the elevator for the Council Chamber when he watched her flowchart all of the systems for a bullying, condescending executive. He was obviously very much her senior, yet he was having great difficulty grasping the breadth of her thinking.

"What if you can't identify the pattern in your past savantflow events. How else might you determine your savant formula?"

"Your *spontaneous-knowledge theme*," called someone from the audience but Connor couldn't see whom it was. "Determine the theme of the activities you were doing when you experienced breakthroughs, epiphanies, coincidences and other spontaneous knowledge events.

"Exactly," said Connor. Other ways of determining your savant formula?

Kellin stood up, "Your *unpaid-work theme*. This entails an examination of the events in your past when you've done work that you crave so much that you'd do it for free. You love it that much. Whereas, others would charge for it because they consider it work. You should be able to trace this theme in patterns of events in your past.

"You'll have emotional highs when you're doing this kind of work so the *positive-emotions theme* will also apply. When you do it, there'll also be the expected occurrences of spontaneous knowledge, flashes of genius, breakthroughs, and clusters of coincidences.

"This is exactly right, Kellin. You've lived your savant formula, haven't you – since you made the car that died on your front lawn operational in your pre-teen years." Kellin nodded.

"What's the difference between breakthroughs, coincidences, spontaneous knowledge and epiphanies," Connor continued.

Kellin, still standing, responded. "Nothing. They're all re-combinations of information systems inside of you or outside of you to invent a new information system. They're all part of the larger scheme of the creative evolutionary advance of the bioflow. Nature can't always solve evolutionary challenges in a gradual incremental way. It must use quantum leaps to create a human eye for example. We want to harness the bioflow's creativity production line to solve the crises of our world."

"Excellent, Kellin," Connor beamed. I never specifically stated that they were all part of the same continuum that connects our inner systems and brain to the bioflow or that they are simply an extension of nature's own universal creative, adaptive, evolutionary process, but you figured it out.

"You're obviously going to excel at exploiting the bioflow for your projects, Kellin. Just as you see how the systems of this huge Government Complex run, you have the expanded consciousness to grasp how the systems of the universe interconnect and operate."

Connor wanted to ensure that KahlDahr Kellin, Rolland, Olivia and others were not intimidated by those with multiple degrees or from more elevated castes. He wanted them free to create and achieve at the maximum of their significant talents.

Connor was a big Kellin fan. The KahlDahr was so incredibly talented. He was also good people. The two had a special bond.

They both shared a wisdom that comes from living from unity consciousness and seeing how everything is connected, even the two of them. He had a warm spot in his heart for Olivia and Kellin's son, Rolland, for the same reason.

Rolland was still working on his biology degree, yet his expansive brilliance was more insightful than mature professionals in that field. He could see biological systems as ingeniously as his father could see mechanical systems or Liv could see programming systems. All three had effortlessly absorbed the systems thinking underlying savanting.

"You've created a quantum leap for everyone, Kellin. In savantflow, your concentration is simply on the creative act you are doing. You become pure creation. This is our natural state. This is nature's natural state. This is my process of savanting in a nutshell.

"Let's say you've never been free during your life to discover your unpaid work theme. What other patterns of events in your past could you track to determine your savant formula?" No one responded. "How else could you get into savantflow within the bioflow?" No one responded. "What other themes could you follow?" No one responded.

He had told them that all of the themes point to the same savant formula, so perhaps they thought learning only one or two would be enough. However, being fluent in them all means that you'll be able to action incoming events in your life more quickly. You'll make directional decisions faster.

"We've identified the *savantflows theme* or *savantflow-bioflow theme*, the *spontaneous-knowledge theme*, the *unpaid-work theme*, and the *positive-emotions theme*. What else?"

Finally, Henerik Halderson posited an answer. "You can look at the events of new knowledge that you naturally pursued since childhood."

When they recruited him, Henerik was a biochemistry degree dropout seeking to find himself and his purpose. Henerik had blossomed with the Breakthru Mission and School. He had found his purpose.

"Yes, good," reinforced Connor. "You want to assess the common thread of any new learning that you voluntarily sought. Your *learning-pursuit theme* or *knowledge-pursuit theme*.

Henerik nodded before continuing, "What growth have you sought historically? Your *growth theme* or *growth-pursuit theme*. What is the theme that runs through the times in your past when you were creative or inventive? And what is the common territory of new creations that you've historically sought? Your *creativity theme* or *creation theme*? Also, in what fields did you choose to be creative? What is your *creativity-pursuit theme*?

"And what is the commonality of the new territories of knowledge or new frontiers that you've historically penetrated? Your *frontier-pursuit theme*. These are all likely to also generate emotional highs so, as Kellin indicated, you could also track what work or activities generated passion, excitement, and enthusiasm. Your *positive-emotions theme*."

"Good work, Henerik! You've added a number of categories of past events to our list for assessment. There are a couple more that offer alternative means to identify your savant formula. Anyone? Yes, Marta."

Marta Kaase was a Varunian electrical engineer also laid off from the power plants like fellow-Varunian Sibylla. Connor had learned that in the Annutia caste system, Varunians were one step above the KahlDahr and one rung below the Azurites.

"Your *successful-projects theme*," suggested Marta. "I think we could pick our future projects based on our past successful projects – ones with the tell-tale arrows that everyone has been identifying."

"You're exactly right, Marta. When you're choosing your projects for the Breakthru Mission, you'll want to ensure you capitalize on the formula that has created successful projects in your past. Now that you know about the bioflow, you don't want to see those projects as isolated events. There is a pattern. If you can dig for it, there is no need to ever pursue a project that will not succeed again. Never again will you swim upstream against the bioflow to try to make a project work.

"We know if it's a right project for us that we will see clusters of coincidences, breakthroughs and other spontaneous knowledge events, facilitating events and gates, emotional highs, and serial savantflows. Marta, what will we see if we choose projects not on the yellow-brick road, so to speak?"

"Blocks," said Marta. "Setbacks. Negative emotions. The absence of any arrows or signposts. Hard work step-by-step instead of coincidences and facilitating events catapulting you forward hundreds of steps at a time.

"You'll have to use discipline to push yourself to keep going instead of being pulled forward by compelling drives. The formula of past failed projects will continue in the future. There is now a predictability that never existed for me before. There appears to be an incredible order to reality where we assumed chaos."

"Precisely," said Connor. "Well done, Marta. I've asked you all to start developing hypotheses as to what projects you want to pursue to solve the planet's crises. When you test them out, if they're wrong for you or the planet or the evolutionary bioflow of the planet, Marta has described precisely what you'll experience. You'll then need to quickly replace those projects.

"We can do your first test right now. When you think of doing the project you have selected, are you excited or does your energy nosedive? That is your first indication. Are you going to have to push yourself to do the wrong project rather than being joyfully excited by the right project? Excellent work, Marta."

"Who has remembered the last two themes or patterns of past events that you can evaluate?" probed Connor further.

Sven Steensen called out, "Your historical meaning theme or *meaning-pursuit theme*. What projects, work, or contributions have historically given your life meaning. What contributions do you crave to make?"

Sven was a mechanical engineer. Like Sibylla Lund and Marta Kaase, he was also laid off from a hydropower company as they had to return to burning fossil fuels.

"Thank you, Sven. Obviously, we need everyone doing work that is meaningful to them. This is part of the positive-emotions theme when you're on the right path to maximization and immersion into the bioflow.

What is the last theme to identify one's savant formula? Jordaan, what is the one we're missing? The most elusive one until you develop this skill?"

"Resonance. Your pattern or *theme of resonance events*," exclaimed Jordaan Jostad after a moment of pensive reflection. An astrophysicist, Jordaan is adept at applying the laws of physics and chemistry to explain the birth, life and death of stars, planets, galaxies, nebulae and other objects in the universe.

This was the perfect direction for someone who'd been addicted to the pursuit of astronomy and cosmology since his childhood years with his Dad, a world-renowned astronomer. Much to his surprise, his Dad was all in favor of Jordaan participating in the Breakthru Mission. Connor learned why at a social event at Axl's home.

Apparently, Dad attributes his own success to an incredible memory and the logic to apply that knowledge. While they were both passionate about the same fields, these were not Jordaan's strengths. He showed signs of being much more inventive, imaginative, and creative. Jordaan had a gift for inventing new scientific equipment and designing unprecedented computer software to analyze data and such. Dad's strengths were left-brain; his son's were right-brain.

Dad had realized when Connor selected his son that he'd recruited the right strengths for the Annutia Breakthru Mission. He felt Commander Kane could teach Jordaan things that he could not. That Kane could cultivate in his son strengths that he himself did not possess.

Because Jostad Sr, believed so much in Connor, he had secured additional funding for the program to ensure its success. Connor was pleased to have a creative as talented as Jordaan in the group.

"You are exactly right," confirmed Connor. "Tell us about resonance and how to use it, Jordaan."

"This is our frequency-sensing ability. You are one tuning fork. When you concentrate on a direction option which is the right one to take towards maximization within the maximization direction of the bioflow, it's like a second tuning fork starts to tone in resonance with you, the first tuning fork. This is how you can proceed quickly and safely into unknown territory.

"You look at your list of possible directions and choose the one where you feel the surge of a second tuning fork beginning to cause vibration within you in resonance."

"Is resonance the same as gut feel or intuition, Jordaan?

"No, sir. It has no additional information other than two things having the same frequency."

"Precisely. Well done. Thank you, Jordaan." Connor went to turn away and then turned back to ask as an afterthought, "Have you ever used your resonance, Jordaan?"

"No, sir."

"Raise your hands. Who has used resonance or thinks they have? About 20%. I suspect that within a couple of months, most of you will raise your hands. Resonance or frequency-sensing is faster in determining direction. It means you won't have to test various direction hypotheses to look for other indicator events in your reality before you can determine your best direction in which to proceed.

"Now, what if you don't have the patterns of events of any of these themes in your past. A *no-themes* situation. What does that mean? What should you do? Yes, Mikael?"

"This means you've lived your life directed by external elements – you've been externally referenced – rather than complying with your natural addictive drives internally – or been internally referenced. Consequently, you haven't maximized. Therefore, you haven't merged with the bioflow. As a result, you'll have less consistent patterns or fewer of them to help you to determine direction to achieve your goals. You won't be able to recruit the power of the bioflow."

Connor was pleased that Mikael had taken his attention off Dania long enough to participate. Mikael was brilliantly creative, perhaps the best after Kellin. Connor knew when he recruited him that he was going to excel at using savanting to solve the crises. Since then he'd proven even better than expected.

Mikael was another brilliant Varunian bench-pressing out of his caste. That he should have had difficulty finding work was such a waste of extraordinary talent. Connor was grateful for his availability to contribute to the Breakthru Mission.

"So, what do you need to do, Mikael?"

"Start savanting with serial savantflows so that the indicators will emerge. Then you can use them to predict your future and your ideal direction."

"Exactly, Mikael. However, I'll give you all a hint. None of you are in this 'no-themes' category. You were recruited based on your themes of past events in your life and their match to the planetary crises.

"Good work, everyone!" Connor praised. I'm going to give you the rest of today to analyze your past patterns of events to help you to pick out at least one project that has the greatest chance of success. Know your savant formula. Then use that formula to select the projects that you would be most excited to pursue to save Annutia."

APPENDIX III: Reset to your Maximum

Excerpt from *BioMaxed*: Chapters 30 and 31, *Reset to your Maximum* by Lauren Holmes (2019)

RESET SCENARIOS for the EMPLOYED
to reset to their maximum by achieving sustained or serial top-talent *flow*

These scenarios suggest contexts conducive to releasing you to reintegrate with nature's adaptation machinery. Once you begin moving in the direction of your maximum, there will come a point of critical mass. Nature will take over and begin pulling you to your maximum and into adaptive directions. Nature's maximizing machinery will begin grouping your system to advantage for synergies and synchronizing. For those who are employed, it is still possible to free yourself to reset to your maximum. Where possible, however, you should keep risks to your current employment status to a minimum until your expertise develops.

Scenario 1:   Redesign your existing job

If employed, your ideal method to reset to your maximum is to re-design your existing job to comply with your natural growth path and the direction the maximizing machinery has historically pressured your system to progress. If this cannot be done directly, perhaps the following strategies might be used:

- Add special projects to your job, especially skunkworks or new ventures. Top-talent *flow* can only be experienced if you are advancing through new challenges and creations.
- Join projects elsewhere within your employer

- Partner with companies that do business with your employer or create projects around the interface
- Create charitable ventures for your employer's corporate giving program which require your strongest talents
- Seek secondments to governments or companies/organizations surrounding your employer which will benefit both sides and you.

Scenario 2:   Take a different job that already exists within your current employer
Scenario 3:   Create a new job within your employer
Scenario 4:   Create a new project or new venture within your current employer
Ideally these will become part of your existing job as part of the job redesign sought in Scenario 1. However, if necessary, work outside of your job on perhaps initially unsanctioned projects until they have advanced enough to be supported by your employer and become part of your job or create a new job ideal for you.

Scenario 5:   Take an active Board of Director position with an outside company
This will let you do the work you were designed to do without leaving your employer.

Scenario 6:   Work for a charity or not-for-profit after work
Ideally this could be a role sponsored by your current employer as part of their corporate giving program identified in the redesign of your job in Scenario 1. However, it may be necessary to create a new context conducive to resetting to your maximum which is unrelated to your current job or employer.

Caution: For the goals of this exercise, it is important to not be dragged into work which is not related to resetting your system to its maximum. Unfortunately, one must recognize that the needs of the have-nots in this world are infinite. You are taking on this additional work to reset to your maximum in a meaningful way. It is best to restrict the gift you are prepared to give to the giving of your strongest talents applied to your most rewarding and valued work at your maximum. This benefits both sides of the equation while energizing rather than depleting you. The resulting partnership with the maximizing machinery will reposition you to a more adaptive context long-term.

Scenario 7: Cultivate a hobby outside of work in which you can maximize

There is the possibility that breakthrough synthesis may find a way for your hobby or home studies to eventually become your source of revenue and ultimately your career. Remember to choose your hobbies to comply with your unpaid work drives, and creation-pursuit, growth-pursuit, frontiering-pursuit, and top-talent *flow* drives. So many fabulous careers have been launched in a home garage.

Scenario 8: Research projects undertaken for your employer

These projects should comply with your knowledge-pursuit, creation-pursuit, and frontiering-pursuit drives. Achieving breakthroughs that will advance your employer or your industry will advance your career, upgrade your worth to your employer, and become the driver of your biologically maximized career. So many phenomenal careers have begun with a single breakthrough.

Scenario 9:   Give Speeches. Write books. Blog. Teach. Pursue a field of study

The preparation and delivery of material you are passionate about developing within the territory of your strongest talents will pull you into serial top-talent *flow* states. This will give you access to the magic associated with coupling with the maximizing machinery and its serial breakthrough synthesis. Even a few breakthroughs may be career-changing, life-changing, and even world-changing.

APPENDIX III: Reset to your Maximum

Excerpt from BioMaxed: Chapters 30 and 31, *Reset to your Maximum* by Lauren Holmes (2019)

RESET SCENARIOS for the UNEMPLOYED
to reset to their maximum by achieving sustained or serial top-talent *flow*

This collection of scenarios for resetting to your maximum capitalizes on the increased flexibility of the unemployed. The scenarios are grouped into two categories:

Scenarios 1-4: This set of contexts for biologically normalizing include assembling a company, buying a company, starting a company, or borrowing a company or job

Scenarios 5-7: This second category of scenarios is fashioned directly from the seven iconic founders of Google, Facebook, Microsoft, Apple, and Amazon we have been examining in earlier articles. It is about releasing to your natural drives for growth, creation, frontiering™, and learning until you are able to commercialize them into paid play, often with the creation of a new field or frontier. This is the means to achieve your maximum lifetime legacy and really explore the outer limits of your capabilities.

Scenario 1: Assemble a mature virtual company from existing components: companies, firms, professionals, technology, information systems, contractors, consultants, workforces, skills, and such.

This is one of my favorite techniques for quickly resetting my outplacement clients to their maximum to accelerate their job search process. A virtual organization is assembled to provide the perfect context to replicate one's past maximum events.

It should therefore comply with your findings from your *sourcing-your-savant* exercise: your unpaid work, creation-pursuit, frontier-pursuit, and core-expansion themes and especially your historical formula for top-talent flow. Anything that does not help you to persist in serial top-talent flow states is outsourced. Anything that is more work than play is outsourced.

Virtual company design

This scenario is not about starting and growing an entrepreneurial company from scratch. This is about melding fully operational units together as a mature company. Nor should this model be used to recreate a lost job. The job was lost due to system corrections which may well have been instigated by the adaptivity needs of your own system. There is little future in trying to go against the flow of the maximizing process.

The maximizing machinery found your de-hiring adaptive for some human system whether that system was yours, the company's, the market's, the industry's, or some other system. There had to be many thwarting signals consistent with no support by the maximizing machinery that you had to overlook to end up experiencing the surprise loss of your job.

Now that you know what to look for, you will not be blindsided again. In the future, you will proactively reposition with the signposts of the maximizing machinery to be led out of the old context and into a new more adaptive one.

Coincidences, breakthroughs, flow events, and quantum leaps will catapult you nonlinearly and opportunistically to endgame jobs or the success of this newly created customized virtual organization. When you have the right design for your system, the virtual company will almost form itself.

There will be magic. There should be lots of leaps propelling your forward. So even if you have only an emotional blueprint of the final company design or how it will feel, you can move at top speed to implement it. Partnering with the maximizing machinery will ensure that your natural growth path will become the company's growth path.

The virtual company is intrinsically rewarding in and of itself. However, it will also be one of the fastest ways to penetrate the *hidden job market* to close your ideal job. This will require a separate article to explain. Suffice it to say that your marketing efforts for selling your virtual company's services will coincide with selling yourself into your ideal job.

Scenario 2: Buy a company with private equity

You may not need to create a virtual organization to reset to your maximum. You may be lucky enough to find a company that will give you your ideal job for operating at your biological maximum and you can simply buy the company. Look for flows to facilitate finding the right company and blocks to the wrong one.

Scenario 3: Start an entrepreneurial company along your natural growth path

The design of the company should offer the perfect expression of the maximum you. The growth path of the company should align with your knowledge-pursuit, creation-pursuit, frontiering-pursuit and core-expansion or growth drives. The goal is to be paid to achieve your maximum lifetime growth and achievement.

Scenario 4: Borrow a company and/or a job

An interim employment contract is a great way to normalize to your maximum. Employment could be at a company, a not-for profit, an association, a charity, or similar. If there are no interim executive jobs available, it may be advantageous to offer your services for free to speed your reset to your maximum. Coincidences and breakthroughs may then quickly catapult you to a more permanent arrangement.

Scenario 5: Free-form work driven by your unleashed top-talent drives: *Unpaid-work* and *knowledge-pursuit*, *creation-pursuit*, *frontiering-pursuit*, *core-expansion*, and *top-talent flow* drives

This is a completely unstructured approach to freeing your day to the above drives in order to advance the world in some way. This is intrinsically rewarding in and of itself. However, over time you will begin to scale new frontiers in your top-talent territory. A plethora of breakthroughs, coincidences, and leaps will pull you in unknown directions which in 20/20 hindsight will appear immensely logical and adaptive. You will find that your version of Amazon, Google, Microsoft, Facebook, or Apple will emerge.

This is a frontiering adventure into new territory or bringing the new into existence. It is pure serial breakthrough synthesis. Rather than having a defined structure for a project or entrepreneurial company, this is about being pulled by the drives and passions associated with applying one's strongest talents until the field, the job, the invention, the discovery, or the company emerges.

Scenario 6: Analyzing and developing your 'science'
This is not about true science. This is about the development of a set of rules or procedures or discoveries that will allow those without your innate talent to operate as you do or to accomplish goals you were able to accomplish. You are seeing my *science* in these articles. They capture what I do instinctively so that others without my aptitude may apply it to achieve beyond their potential. As you analyze how you use your strongest talents you will be increasing your abilities and breaking through new frontiers. For some, this scenario will allow them to achieve top-talent *flow* states and reset to their maximum. It will work for the employed or unemployed.

Scenario 7: Pursue your lifetime legacy
There are those who know what they want their greatest lifetime legacy to be based on the maximum application of their strongest talents applied to the most worthy cause for the most receptive and valuing audience. By committing to its achievement using the breakthrough synthesis of the maximizing machinery, you will quickly find that you have reset to your maximum.

ABOUT THE AUTHOR

Lauren Holmes is CEO of Frontiering, a company dedicated to creating biologically maximized careers which ensure intrinsically rewarding work, peak achievement, self-actualization, self-transcendence, and profound purpose and meaning.

Lauren has developed an unprecedented savant-inspired protocol called *savanting* to enable individuals to achieve at their highest potential. The methodology was first identified when Lauren interviewed 300 successful C-Suite executives and Board members of global companies in a compressed period of time as CEO of an executive search firm.

Their shared modus operandi through the lens of her degree in biological anthropology from University of Toronto yielded a new formula for career, life, leadership, and entrepreneurial success. A new level of human potential was identified.

The protocol was perfected over two decades of experimentation with global executives – first through executive coaching, then through executive career management, and now through the co-creation of contexts customized to biological strengths. These contexts include new companies, projects, ventures, frontiers, or redesigned jobs through which the client will excel.

Lauren is an award-winning author of fiction and nonfiction books based on demonstrating her self-actualizing protocol in action: *Peak Evolution: Beyond Peak Performance and Peak Experience* (2001/2010), *The Encore: A Transformational Thriller* (2018), *BioMaxed* (2019), and *Savanting: Outperforming your Potential* (2019).

See LaurenHolmes.com for more about Lauren's books and articles. She may be reached through LaurenHolmes.com/contact or frontiering.com.

CPSIA information can be obtained
at www.ICGtesting.com
Printed in the USA
LVHW090042150120
643683LV00007B/41